P9-DTF-302

HORIZON

JULY, 1960 · VOLUME II, NUMBER 6

HORIZON

A Magazine of the Arts

JULY, 1960 · *VOLUME II, NUMBER 6*

HORIZON is published every two months by American Horizon, Inc., a subsidiary of American Heritage Publishing Co., Inc., 551 Fifth Avenue, New York 17, N. Y.
Single Copies: $3.95
Annual Subscriptions: $18.00 in the U.S. & Can.
$19.00 elsewhere

Second-Class postage paid at New York, N.Y.

COVER: Using a palette of hot primary colors and his customary slashing brushwork, painter Richard Diebenkorn was trying to evoke on canvas the noonday glare of mid-summer. And the big, bold result, with its amusing hint of flags and bunting, is called —what else?—*July*. Like two other San Francisco artists, David Park and Elmer Bischoff, Diebenkorn painted for several years in the abstract expressionist manner. Now, with their styles loosened up and their colors ablaze, all three have abandoned the purely abstract to paint the human figure and the California landscape. An article on this rising trio, together with a portfolio of their work in color gravure, begins on page 16. *July* is in the collection of Martha Jackson.

FRONTISPIECE: Only the most ungrateful and unimaginative bird would rebel against a cage as fantastic and unconfining as this one. Happily, its occupant more than measures up. He is a clever Brazilian parrot named Lucien, who appears in *Orestes, or the Art of Smiling*—a fairy tale written and illustrated by the young Italian artist Domenico Gnoli (HORIZON, July, 1959). This colored drawing of Lucien's giddy cage is in the collection of Mr. and Mrs. Zachary Scott.

THEN: J. Pierpont Morgan the elder brandishes his cane at a news photographer in 1910.

CULVER SERVICE

PRIVACY LOST

© PHILIPPE HALSMAN

NOW: Vice President Nixon obligingly jumps for photographer Philippe Halsman in 1957.

From the picture window it was only a step—and we took it—to TV cameras in the living room and a press agent in the boudoir

By WILLIAM K. ZINSSER

The exact moment when privacy began going out of American life has never been fixed by scholars. Perhaps it was the day when Chic Young, creator of "Blondie," first put Dagwood in the bathtub. Since then countless children and dogs, trooping in and out of Dagwood's bathroom, have sailed little boats in the water where he sat soaping. And countless real children (and dogs) have copied the custom, assuming it to be common behavior. Thus one of modern man's last sanctuaries has been invaded and despoiled.

Invading other people's privacy is now a big pursuit—and big business—in the United States. So is the voluntary surrender of privacy, judging by the large number of men and women who seem driven to make an outward show of their inner selves. Magazines, newspapers, and television programs are battening as never before on the personal lives of the famous, and no detail is too intimate to be made public, as President Eisenhower found during his recovery from a heart attack. In fact, anyone who tries to guard his privacy is regarded as somewhat odd and un-American.

Certainly a man's home is no longer his castle, or, if it is, the moat is dry and the portcullis is always up. Nothing can stanch the daily tide of impersonal mail, peddlers at the door, and strangers on the telephone. In the hands of the inconsiderate the telephone is a deadly weapon, but if a man dons armor against it, by refusing to have his number listed in the directory, he must now pay a penalty. The New York Telephone Company had 400,000 of these recalcitrants on its rolls the first of the year—a figure which suggests that the urge for privacy is still alive, even if the respect for it is not. Recently the company became impatient with its unlisted subscribers and clapped an extra charge on their monthly bill, hoping thereby to force them back into the listed world of good fellowship.

Modern architecture has done its share to banish privacy. The picture window was first designed by men like Frank Lloyd Wright to frame a scene of natural beauty. Today millions of Americans look out of picture windows into other picture windows and busy streets. The building contractor has no sooner finished installing the picture window than the decorator is called in to cover it with expensive curtains against an inquisitive world. Even then, privacy is uncertain. In many modern houses, rooms have yielded to "areas" that merge into each other, so that the husband trying to work in the "reading area" (formerly den) is naked to the blasts from the "recreation area" (formerly rumpus room) a few feet away.

If privacy is hard to find at home, it is almost extinct outside the home. Strangers in the next seat on trains and planes are seldom given to vows of silence, and certainly the airline pilot is no man to leave his passengers to their thoughts. His jovial voice crackles out of the intercom at periodic intervals—generally just when his listeners are dozing off—to impart the latest statistics on ground speed, cruising altitude, and cabin pressure, or to point out "an unusually clear view of Keokuk out the left window." Airplanes have also been infested by canned music, leaving the captive audience aloft no means of escaping and still living to tell the tale. Back on the ground, to find a restaurant, store, railroad station, or bus terminal that doesn't burble with unceasing melody is not easy, nor is it always possible to escape by boarding a bus or taking a walk in the park. Transistor radios, carried everywhere by rock-'n'-roll addicts, have changed all that.

If there is one place where a person might expect a decent quietude, it is his doctor's office. Yet RCA is planning a radio network that will pipe canned music and pharmaceutical commercials to 25,000 doctors in eighteen big cities. This raises a whole new criterion for choosing the family physician. Better to have a second-rate healer content with the sound of his stethoscope than an eminent specialist poking to the rhythms of Gershwin.

Not even nature is a sure refuge. A plan is now afoot to project advertisements on mountainsides and low-lying clouds. Then there are the roars and vapor trails left by jet planes overhead. Just when a man is savoring God's unblemished sky and peace, these thunders and slender ribbons remind him that our defense posture is shaky, that generals are squabbling in the Pentagon, and that Joseph Alsop foresees nothing but doom.

It is not surprising that Americans no longer think twice about invading the privacy of others. Popular example has demolished the very concept, as anyone with a TV set will attest. In this vast medium few secrets are withheld for the sake of modesty and taste. Dr. Joyce Brothers has a program on which she answers such questions as "My husband rarely

Privacy's Rear Guard

Randolph Churchill's finest hour may well have been the moment he told a TV inquisitor ("Night Beat") that he never discussed family affairs with total strangers.

Above: Holding the clamorous reporters at bay on the eve of his wedding, young Steven Rockefeller drew a line between freedom of the press and the privacy of the individual—and made it stick.

Right: Film actress Maureen O'Hara is one of the few celebrities who refused to be terrorized by Confidential *magazine. She sued for a million dollars, won settlement.*

has sexual intercourse with me—what's wrong with him?" Jack Paar, who kneels nightly at the shrine of catharsis on the air waves, had no trouble early this year in finding a riposte against columnist Walter Winchell on the evening of his lachrymose return from exile. Appealing to the audience's sympathy with many a jab at the wicked bosses who had curbed him, he said that Winchell had defamed him and even questioned his virility. "As a moral man," Paar declaimed, "only my wife knows about my virility," and with this touching domestic vignette he routed the foe from darkest Hearstland.

Mike Wallace first achieved fame as a television inquisitor who left no question unasked. To Drew Pearson, for instance, he said: "President Roosevelt once called you a chronic liar; President Truman called you an S.O.B. at one time and a vicious liar at another time. . . . Could it be that you *are* a liar?"

"People's thresholds are lower than they used to be," Wallace remarks, explaining why such questions are tolerated. Nor does TV fix its peeping eye only on the famous. Program hosts ooze familiarity, no matter who comes into their net, and sooner or later almost everybody does. How many wretched women have been induced to bare their miseries on "Queen for a Day"? How many couples have opened their marital troubles to dissection on "Divorce Court"? Small legions have allowed such retrospective shows as "This Is Your Life" and "It Could Be You" to conjure up spirits from their unhappy past.

But no program is so symbolic of the times as Edward R. Murrow's house-visit hour, "Person to Person." In seven years, 550 men and women of varying degrees of prominence have welcomed this program's 19,000,000 viewers into their homes. They have included four Cabinet members, two Supreme Court justices, three college presidents, one archbishop, two bishops, visiting heads of government like U Nu of Burma, foreign diplomats of highest rank, governors and mayors, congressmen and judges, generals and admirals, one ex-President and one ex-King of England.

"It was very rare for people to refuse on the grounds that it was an invasion of their privacy," says former producer Jesse Zousmer. Most men and women were longing to be asked, and many who first declined later changed their minds. "It became a question of prestige to be on it," Zousmer says, "sort of like being invited to the White House."

While TV programs have thus invaded the privacy of men and women as a whole, TV commercials have gone after them limb by limb, and by now they have eroded most of the defenses that once surrounded the human body. When a toddler is old enough to turn a knob, he can see women flexing around the room in girdles and "undies" or rejoicing in the thrust of a new brassière. He can watch them spray deodorants or dab depilatories on themselves in a state of unaccountable rapture, or affix corn plasters to their tortured feet. Meanwhile, inside their transilluminated systems, little Mr.

CONTINUED ON PAGE 120

Publicity's Vanguard

Scores of prominent persons—James Roosevelt is only one—have eagerly exposed themselves to Mike Wallace's third degree on television.

Linda Christian and Tyrone Power had themselves painted seminude, later sold portraits at public auction.

Five days a week, unhappy housewives parade their woes before a TV camera on "Queen for a Day" (those visibly pregnant have an advantage).

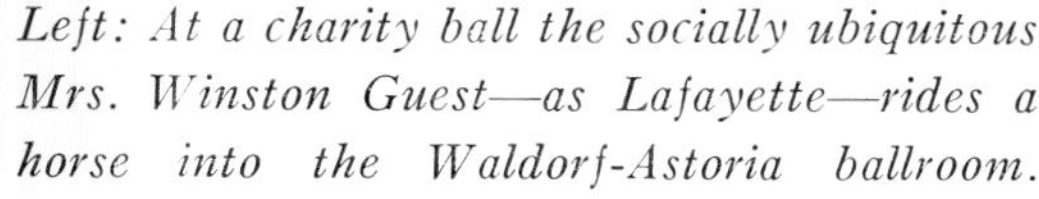

Left: At a charity ball the socially ubiquitous Mrs. Winston Guest—as Lafayette—rides a horse into the Waldorf-Astoria ballroom.

Above: Count Lanfranco Rasponi (seen with Mrs. Lorraine Manville Dresselhuys) is a press agent who specializes in society accounts.

Right: Two figures in the international set who are their own best press agents—the Marquis de Cuevas and Elsa Maxwell (as Sancho Panza).

OPPOSITE: MAX PETER HAAS, BLACK STAR, UPI; GARY WAGNER, UPI, WIDE WORLD PHOTO

THE COMING FLOOD OF PHARAOH'S TEMPLES

I met a traveler from an antique land
Who said: Two vast and trunkless legs of stone
Stand in the desert. Near them, on the sand,
Half sunk, a shattered visage lies, whose frown,
And wrinkled lip, and sneer of cold command,
Tell that its sculptor well those passions read
Which yet survive (stamped on these lifeless things),
The hand that mocked them and the heart that fed;
And on the pedestal these words appear:
"My name is Ozymandias, king of kings;
Look on my works, ye Mighty, and despair!"
Nothing beside remains. Round the decay
Of that colossal wreck, boundless and bare
The lone and level sands stretch far away.

Contrary to the intelligence conveyed by the traveler of Shelley's sonnet, much besides the cold visage toppled to the sands of Thebes remains of the mighty works of Ozymandias. For Ozymandias—User-maat-Re—is more familiarly remembered as Ramses II, the greatest builder of ancient Egypt. This Pharaoh, for whom the children of Israel toiled in bondage, ruled longer than any other—sixty-three years, from 1298 to 1235 B.C. The monuments he left behind were as numerous as his sons, who numbered more than one hundred. He built for the ages, arrogantly razing the monuments of his predecessors for building materials and, where an edifice pleased him, adding his name to it.

In addition to his magnificent mortuary temple, the Rameseum, at Thebes, before which his battered colossus still lies, he built the noble hypostyle hall at Karnak, the great temple at Tanis, and the lofty pylon at Luxor (where, too, he erected the obelisk whose twin stands in the Place de la Concorde). Of all his works, the best preserved is Abu Simbel. There, beside the Nile, in Nubia, between the first and second cataracts, he caused two adjoining temples to be hewn from the living sandstone cliffs. Upon first seeing Abu Simbel, one hundred years ago—its soaring façade then half-buried in sand—the French author Maxime du Camp wrote in awe: "Try to imagine the cathedral of Notre Dame carved out of a single block of stone."

For more than three millennia, Abu Simbel has survived the ravages of desert winds and sands. But about 1970 it is due to vanish forever, along with almost two hundred lesser monuments, beneath the waters of the Nile. The new Aswan dam will create a lake stretching south through the Nubian valley of the Nile for 300 miles, partly in Egypt and partly in the Sudan. It will be 330 feet deep at the dam, 195 feet higher than the flood level of the existing dam at Aswan. The part that lies in Egypt will cover not only Abu Simbel but several other rock-cut and free-standing temples of Ramses II, various tombs, temples, and fortresses of the New Kingdom, and a number of Graeco-Roman temples, some of which were converted to churches by early Christians. Beneath the Sudanese section of the lake will lie at least one hundred sites of archaeological interest, including four Pharaonic temples, rock tombs of the Egyptian Eighteenth Dynasty, early Christian churches, some fourteen fortresses dating from the nineteenth century B.C., and a large number of prehistoric burial places.

The fate of these monuments may be previewed at the island of Philae, near Aswan, where a complex of Ptolemaic and Roman temples has been submerged for nine months of every year since 1902 by the waters of the present dam (see pages 14 and 15). What the periodic attack of water can do may be seen even more clearly in the ruins of the small tem-

Prophetic of the fate in store for many of the great antiquities of Nubia is the half-submerged sphinx at Wadi es-Sebua (opposite). Already under water for much of the year when the lake formed by the present Aswan dam backs up, it will be lost forever when the new dam at Aswan is completed.

C. DESROCHES-NOBLECOURT

ple at Kertassi (see the photograph on pages 12–13).

In hopes of saving the finest of the Nubian monuments from inundation, the United Nations Educational, Scientific, and Cultural Organization has launched a campaign of rescue. The plan calls for building dikes around the two chief sites, at an estimated cost of $4,000,000 for Philae and $30,000,000 to $60,000,000 for Abu Simbel. Some smaller monuments would be dismantled and moved to new sites. From others the most important sculptures and paintings and inscriptions would be removed, while lesser works would be copied and preserved by UNESCO teams. The whole enterprise, experts believe, would cost above $100,000,000, or a fifth of the cost of the dam itself.

HORIZON has requested Etienne Drioton, dean of French Egyptologists, Director General of the Department of Egyptian Antiquities at Cairo until 1952, and presently professor at the Sorbonne, to describe Abu Simbel and its wonders. His account follows in a translation by Willard R. Trask.

ABU SIMBEL: THE SEAL ON THE GATE OF EGYPT

By ETIENNE DRIOTON

For the generation before mine, the temple of Philae was still the pearl of Egypt.

My teacher, Georges Bénédite, who copied its inscriptions in 1887 and 1888, ten years before the building of the first Aswan dam was begun, often spoke of Philae as one of the most remarkable experiences of his life. He would describe his feeling of enchantment each time he crossed the grim granite-rock desert of Aswan and came within sight of the sacred island of Isis. There stood the temple of the goddess, its pylons, porticoes, and kiosks reflected in the blue waters of the Nile, surrounded by palms and acacias. It was, Bénédite said, the vision of Paradise for one emerging from Hell.

Although the beauties of Philae have been drowned for much of every year, now they will be brought down altogether by the ebb and flow of the waters that will be released from the new dam just up-river from the isle. Consigned to oblivion are the small temple of Nectanebo II (359–341 B.C.), the graceful kiosk of the Roman emperor Trajan, and the imposing temple of Isis—built on the foundations of earlier monuments, in the third century B.C., during the reigns of Ptolemy II and Ptolemy III, and subsequently embellished during the Roman imperial occupation.

Philae and Abu Simbel differ in both date and character: the significance of Philae is religious, whereas Abu Simbel is political; Philae gives an impression of grace, while Abu Simbel was intended as an affirmation of power. But these two great temple complexes have one thing in common: each is supremely representative of its period. If they should disappear, a gap that nothing could fill would open in the series of Egyptian artistic and historical treasures that have survived to our day.

Abu Simbel lies some 175 miles south of Philae, at the mouth of a long rock corridor through which flow the waters of the Nile. This Dantesque passageway naturally suggests the idea of a gate, and such is the name it still bears: Bab-el-Kalabsha. Where this landscape ends and the Nile banks change their character and become desert plains broken here and there by conical hills that suggest pyramids, it seems quite natural that the Egyptians should have wished to impress the seal of their civilization and power, as they were accustomed to set a seal on the locks of their doors.

This is not the only place in the southern marches of Egypt where the Pharaohs erected temples to their gods to assert spiritual possession of the country, or forts to dominate it politically. Scattered along the banks of the Nile from Philae south to Abu Simbel are temples at Beit el Wali, Gerf Hussein, Wadi es-Sebua, Amada, and Derr (to mention only the most important of the threatened ones); and, south from Abu Simbel, temples at Aksha, Gebel Adda, Buhen, and even at distant Semna, beyond the second cataract, still bear witness to the Egyptian domination of the country from the time of the Pharaohs of the Middle Kingdom (2258–1570 B.C.).

TEXT CONTINUED ON PAGE 14

DOCUMENTATION CENTRE ON ANCIENT EGYPT, CAIRO

GEORGE GERSTER—BLACK STAR

Above is the 108-foot façade of the great temple at Abu Simbel, with four colossal images of Ramses II hewn from the sandstone escarpment. Both this temple and a smaller one built by Ramses for Queen Nefertari are situated immediately alongside the Nile, at left and right of the picture on the opposite page.

The effect of the ebb and flow of dammed-up waters on the foundations of ancient monuments can be judged from the condition of this Roman temple at Kertassi. Built by the emperor Trajan not far above the present dam at Aswan, it has been inundated for part of every year since 1902.

C. DESROCHES-NOBLECOURT

TEXT CONTINUED FROM PAGE 10

But Ramses II, it seems, desired to outdo in magnificence all his predecessors by erecting at the southern entrance to his country monuments worthy of the civilization that Egypt had imposed on the region. For the two temples at Abu Simbel are the only places in Egypt, except for Thebes, where we find such grandiose and colossal architecture.

It is likely that in constructing these extraordinary edifices Ramses II was realizing a dynastic project that had originated when the Nineteenth Dynasty acceded to the throne in 1313 B.C. For a dedicatory inscription carved in the passageway between two inner chambers of the great temple at Abu Simbel is dated in the first year of Ramses II. This suggests that a large part of the work had already been carried out during the reign of his immediate predecessor, Seti I (1312–1298 B.C.).

However this may be, the choice of the site was admirable. Along the west bank of the Nile, south of the gorges of lower Nubia, two immense rounded masses of sandstone plunge almost straight down into the river; between them is a ravine into which the sand flows tirelessly, like a golden stream, from the desert plateau (page 10). The site was well suited to temples of the type already familiar in Nubia: the inner and most important part, containing the sanctuary, was hidden within the mountain, hewn from the living rock; the temple court and outbuildings were set in front, by the riverbank. Hence, in antiquity, the monuments were not entirely visible from the valley, as they have become since the forestructures disappeared. The arriving visitor saw, above the surrounding buildings, only the upper part of the colossi along the temple façades.

The two temples are ranged along the riverbank a short distance apart. The larger, which is to the south, was consecrated by Ramses II to Re-Harmakhis, the Sun; Amon, god of Thebes; Ptah of Memphis, and the deified Ramses II himself. But all four of the 67-foot-high colossi (page 11), carved from the living rock almost in the full round, are actually images of Ramses. Above the temple door, on a level with the heads, a niche is occupied by a colossal figure in high relief, which represents the Sun in the form of a falcon-headed man crowned by a disk. Beside the legs of the colossi, and against the vertical support of their thrones, eight standing statues represent the king's mother, Queen Tui, his wife Nefertari, and some of his daughters; between the colossi's legs are smaller statues representing four other children of Ramses II and Nefertari. Thus the royal family mounts guard at the entrance to the temple.

The first chamber behind the entrance door is a great hall, some 55 feet deep by 50 feet wide, divided into three naves by a double row of eight columns against which stand the same number of 30-foot statues representing the king with his scepters crossed over his breast. The decoration of this hall is of the type usually found on the walls of the first court behind the pylons in free-standing temples. It presents the epic of the royal exploits. On the north wall we find carved in low relief the same repertory of images that elsewhere—especially on the pylons of the temple at Luxor and in the court of the Rameseum—illustrated the campaign by Ramses II against the Hittites in the fifth year of his reign. Here the Pharaoh's pictorial account of the Battle of Kadesh is full and explicit, showing the citadel of Kadesh in a loop of the Orontes River, the Egyptian camp surrounded by a palisade of shields, the thrashing of the false spies, the king in his chariot charging desperately to disengage his army from the ambush into which it had fallen, the cavalry battle, the counting of the prisoners. The other walls confusedly juxtapose representations of Ramses' victories over the Libyans (see page 15), the Nubians, and the Hittites again. The king offers all his enemies together to Re-Harmakhis, the chief patron deity of the temple.

In the following hall, we come to what corresponds to the secret part of free-standing temples. Its decoration is purely religious, showing the Pharaoh and his wife offering incense to the gods. Then a hall of lesser dimensions leads to the sanctuary itself: a chamber 21 feet deep by 12 feet wide, at the back of which the four patron deities of the temple—Re-Harmakhis, Amon, Ptah, and the deified Ramses—are enthroned side by side on one bench.

The adjacent temple of Queen Nefertari is of appropriately smaller dimensions. The six standing colossi along its façade are only 30 feet high. They comprise four representations of Ramses and two of the queen. The interior consists of only two small halls. The ceiling of the first is supported by six Hathoric columns; that is, columns with capitals representing a sistrum, a characteristic Egyptian musical instrument

CONTINUED ON PAGE 124

ALBERT RACCAH—UNESCO

C. DESROCHES-NOBLECOURT

Within the threatened temple of Ramses II at Abu Simbel, the exploits of the Pharaoh are depicted in rich relief cut into the sandstone walls. One carving (above) shows the warrior-king mounted in his chariot, attacking the Libyans. The matching photographs (below) show two stages of the inundation of the temple of Isis on the isle of Philae. The first picture, on the opposite page, shows the water rising on the temple façade after the existing Aswan dam is closed annually in October. When high water is reached in January (below) only the roofs of the buildings break the surface.

ALBERT RACCAH—UNESCO

By ELEANOR C. MUNRO

FIGURES TO THE FORE

Banished by abstract expressionism, the human form has come back —somewhat changed by exile—to the canvases of a California trio

Three San Francisco painters—Elmer Bischoff, David Park, and Richard Diebenkorn—have recently attracted a good deal of attention, partly because of the novel possibility of a new style emerging from the West Coast, and partly for their own distinctive qualities. The new style attributed to them is based upon the human figure, to which all three have come after some years of commitment to abstract expressionism. They still employ the rough brushwork, the thick, overlaid paint surfaces, and the brittle, often acid color contrasts which are called "abstract expressionist" today; but now they are using recognizable figures in their pictures—as a kind of catalyst to make the colors and shapes coalesce into firm relationships. So one is led to ask what precisely *is* new here? And, furthermore, where does this new manifestation lie vis-à-vis the contemporary styles of New York, Paris, and the rest of the world? Are these three artists using tag ends of difficult techniques in a less demanding style, or are they originators of a new language of art?

The artists themselves neither pose the question nor suggest an answer. Taciturn and self-absorbed, they form a beguiling "still point" in the turning world of beatniks and publicity seekers; they enter upon the public stage almost unwillingly, unready to expound very much on their art. Not so young as revolutionaries go (Bischoff is forty-four, Park forty-nine, and Diebenkorn thirty-eight), they are, however, properly lanky and clean-cut in the Western pioneer manner. David Park is the sole outlander of the group, but he left his native Boston long ago and has lived in the Golden State almost continuously since 1929. The three have been more or less closely associated since the mid-1940's, when they were on the faculty of the California School of Fine Arts in San Francisco, then the site of a creative ferment under the aegis of the abstract expressionists Clyfford Still and Mark Rothko. Now among the patriarchs of abstract painting, these two were fierce visionaries and impressive teachers, especially to the uprooted and unsettled members of the faculty and student body then returning from the war. Bischoff, Park, and Diebenkorn were among many swept into their orbit. Still's own transcendental aesthetic underscored the spirit of the place: "Let no man undervalue the implications of this work, or its power for life—or for death, if it is misused." By this abstract expressionist doctrine, each gesture of the artist is a foray into danger, like exploring with a lighted match among chambers of dynamite. It was only after Still and Rothko had decamped for the East that Park, in 1950, then Bischoff in '52 and Diebenkorn in '55, left off this kind of pursuit of power through paint and turned to a more naturalistic kind of art. It may

TEXT CONTINUED ON PAGE 114

STAEMPFLI GALLERY

DAVID PARK, "STANDING COUPLE," 1958

POINDEXTER GALLERY

RICHARD DIEBENKORN, "OCEAN VIEW FROM WINDOW," 1959

POINDEXTER GALLERY

RICHARD DIEBENKORN, "COFFEE," 1959

DAVID PARK, "FOUR MEN," 1958

COLLECTION WHITNEY MUSEUM OF AMERICAN ART, NEW YORK

COLLECTION OF JOSEPH H. HIRSHHORN, COURTESY STAEMPFLI GALLERY

ELMER BISCHOFF, "LANDSCAPE WITH BARE TREE," 1958

STAEMPFLI GALLERY

ELMER BISCHOFF, "TWO FIGURES WITH VERMILION LIGHT," 1959

COLLECTION MUSEUM OF MODERN ART, NEW YORK

ELMER BISCHOFF, "GIRL WADING," 1959

By LOREN EISELEY

NATURE, MAN, and MIRACLE

For centuries man saw himself as the center of a universe that had been created especially for him. After Darwin that was no longer possible: science had made the world seem completely natural, and man's presence in it no more miraculous than that of the beasts he is kin to. But how natural is "natural"? That is the question to which Loren Eiseley addresses himself in his forthcoming book, *The Firmament of Time* (Atheneum), of which this is the final chapter. Here he ventures some comment upon "the world we now call 'natural,' as if, in some manner, we had tamed it sufficiently to include it under the category of 'known and explored,' as if it had little in the way of surprises yet in store for us." As an anthropologist, author, and Provost of the University of Pennsylvania, Mr. Eiseley has never lost his own capacity for surprise or that "sense of awe and marvel . . . without which man would not be man."

In the more obscure scientific circles which I frequent, there is a legend circulating about a late, distinguished physicist who, in his declining years, persisted in wearing enormous padded boots much too large for him. He had developed, it seems, what to his fellows was a wholly irrational fear of falling through the interstices of that largely empty molecular space which common men in their folly speak of as the world. A stroll across his living room floor had become, for him, something as dizzily horrendous as the activities of a window washer on the Empire State Building. Indeed, with equal reason, he could have passed an insubstantial hand through his own body.

The pulsing rivers of his blood, the awe-inspiring movement of his thoughts had become a vague cloud of electrons interspersed with the light-year distances that obtain between us and the farther galaxies. This was the natural world which he had helped to create, and in which, at last, he had found himself a lonely and imprisoned occupant. All around him the ignorant rushed on their way over the illusion of substantial floors, leaping, though they did not see it, from particle to particle over a bottomless abyss. There was even a question as to the reality of the particles that bore them up. It did not, however, keep insubstantial newspapers from being sold or insubstantial love from being made.

Not long ago I became aware of another world, perhaps equally as natural and as real, which man is beginning to forget. My thinking began in Connecticut under a boat dock. The lake I speak of has been pre-empted and "civilized" by man. All day long in the vacation season, high-speed motorboats, driven with the reckless abandon common to the young Apollos of our society, speed back and forth carrying loads of equally attractive girls. The shores echo to the roar of powerful motors and the delighted screams of young Americans with uncounted horsepower surging under their hands. In truth, as I sat there under the boat dock, I had some desire to swim or to canoe in the older ways of the great forest that once lay about this region. Either notion would have been folly. I would have been gaily chopped to ribbons by teenage youngsters whose eyes were always immutably fixed on the far horizons of space or upon the dials which indicated the speed of their passing. There was another world, I was to discover, along the lake shallows and under the boat dock where the motors could not come.

As I sat there one sunny morning when the water was peculiarly translucent, I saw a dark shadow moving swiftly over the bottom. It was the first sign of life I had seen in this lake whose shores seemed to yield little but washed-up beer cans. By and by the gliding shadow ceased to scurry from stone to stone over the bottom. Unexpectedly it headed almost directly for me. A furry nose with gray whiskers broke the surface. Below the whiskers, green water foliage trailed out in an inverted V as long as his body. A muskrat still lived in the lake. He was bringing in his breakfast.

I sat very still in the strips of sunlight under the pier. To my surprise the muskrat came almost to my feet with his little breakfast of greens. He was young, and it rapidly became obvious to me that he was laboring under an illusion of his own, and that he thought animals and men were still living in the Garden of Eden. He gave me a friendly glance from time to time as he nibbled his greens. Once, even, he went out into the lake again and returned to my feet with more greens. He had not, it seemed, heard very much about man. I shuddered. Only the evening before I had heard a man describe with triumphant enthusiasm how he had killed a rat in the garden because the creature had dared to nibble his petunias. He had even shown me the murder weapon, a sharp-edged brick.

On this pleasant shore a war was being waged, and it would go on until nothing remained but man. Yet this creature with the gray, appealing face wanted very little: a strip of shore to coast up and down, sunlight and moonlight, some weeds from the deep water. He was an edge-of-the-world dweller, caught between a vanishing forest and a deep lake pre-empted by unpredictable machines full of chopping blades. He eyed me nearsightedly, a green leaf poised in his mouth. Plainly he had come with some poorly instructed memory about the lion and the lamb.

"You had better run away now," I said softly, making no movement in the shafts of light. "You are in the wrong universe and must not make this mistake again. I am really a very terrible and cunning beast. I can throw stones." With this I dropped a little pebble at his feet.

He looked at me half-blindly, with eyes much better adjusted to the wavering shadows of his lake bottom than to sight in the open air. He made almost as if to take the pebble up in his forepaws. Then a thought seemed to cross his mind —a thought perhaps telepathically received, as Freud once hinted, in the dark world below and before man, a whisper of ancient disaster heard in the depths of a burrow. Perhaps, after all, this was not Eden. His nose twitched carefully; he edged toward the water.

"... the physicist has penetrated the deepest into life. He has come to that place of whirling sparks which are themselves phantoms. He is close upon the void where science ends and the manifestation of God's prerogative begins...."

As he vanished in an oncoming wave, there went with him a natural world, distinct from the world of girls and motorboats, distinct from the world of the professor holding to reality by some great snowshoe effort in his study. My muskrat's shore-line universe was edged with the dark wall of hills on one side and the waspish drone of motors farther out, but it was a world of sunlight he had taken down into the waterweeds. It hovered there, waiting for my disappearance. I walked away obscurely pleased that darkness had not gained on life by any act of mine.

In so many worlds, I thought, how natural is "natural"—and is there anything we can call a natural world at all?

Nature, contended John Donne in the seventeenth century, is the common law by which God governs us. Donne was already aware of the new science and impressed by glimpses of those vast abstractions which man was beginning to build across the gulfs of his ignorance. Donne made, however, a reservation that rings strangely in the modern ear. If nature is the common law, he said, then miracle is God's prerogative.

By the nineteenth century, this spider web of common law had been flung across the deeps of space and time. "In astronomy," meditated Emerson, "vast distance, but we never go into a foreign system. In geology, vast duration, but we are never strangers. Our metaphysics should be able to follow the flying force through all its transformations."

Now admittedly there is a way in which all these worlds are real and sufficiently natural. We can say, if we like, that the muskrat's world is naïve and limited, a fraction, a bare fraction of the world of life: a view from a little pile of wet stones on a nameless shore. The view of the motorboat speedsters is, in essence, similar and no less naïve. All would give way to the priority of that desperate professor striving like a tired swimmer to hold himself aloft against the soft and fluid nothingness beneath his feet. In terms of the modern temper, the physicist has penetrated the deepest into life. He has come to that place of whirling sparks which are themselves phantoms. He is close upon the void where science ends and the manifestation of God's prerogative begins. "He can be no creature," argued Donne, "who is present at the first creation."

Yet there is a way in which the intelligence of man in this era of science and the machine can be viewed as having taken the wrong turning. There is a dislocation of our vision which is, perhaps, the product of the kind of creatures we are, or at least conceive ourselves to be. Man, as a two-handed manipulator of the world about him, has projected himself outward upon his surroundings in a way impossible to other creatures. He has done this since the first half-human man-ape hefted a stone in his hand. He has always sought mastery over the materials of his environment, and in our day he has pierced so deeply through the screen of appearances that the age-old distinctions between matter and energy have been dimmed to the point of disappearance. The creations of his clever intellect ride in the skies and the seas' depths; he has hurled a fragment of metal at the moon, which he once feared. He holds the heat of suns within his hands and threatens with it both the lives and happiness of his unborn descendants.

Man, in the words of one astute biologist, is "caught in a physiological trap and faced with the problem of escaping from his own ingenuity." Pascal, with intuitive sensitivity, saw this at the very dawn of the modern era in science: "There is nothing which we cannot make natural," he wrote, and then, prophetically, comes the full weight of his judgment upon man, "there is nothing natural which we do not destroy." *Homo faber,* Man the Toolmaker, is not enough. There must be another road and another kind of man lurking in the mind of this odd creature, but whether the attraction of that path is as strong as the age-old primate addiction to taking things apart, remains to be seen.

We who are engaged in the life of thought are likely to assume that the key to an understanding of the world is knowledge, both of the past and future—that if we had that knowledge we would also have wisdom. It is not my intention here to decry learning. It is only that we must come to understand the fact that learning is endless and that nowhere does it lead us behind the existent world. It may reduce the prejudices of ignorance, set our bones, build our cities. In itself it will never make us ethical men. Yet because we conceive ours as an age of progress, and because we know more about time and history than any men before us, we fallaciously equate scientific progress with ethical advance in a point-to-point relationship. Thus, as society improves physically, we *assume* the improvement of the individual and are all the more horrified at those mass movements of terror which have so typified the first half of this century.

On another morning of which I am about to speak, I was surfeited with the smell of mortality and tired of the years I had spent in archaeological dustbins. I rode out of a camp and across a mountain. I would never have believed, before it happened, that one could ride into the past on horseback. It is true I rode with a purpose, but that purpose was to settle an argument within myself.

It was time, I thought, to face up to what was in my mind —to the dust and the broken teeth and the spilled chemicals of life seeping away into the sand. It was time I admitted that life was of the earth, earthy, and could be turned into a piece of wretched tar. It was time I consented to the proposition that man had as little to do with his fate as a seed blown against a grating. It was time I looked upon the world without spectacles and saw love and pride and beauty dissolve into effervescing juices. I could be an empiricist with the best of them. I would be deceived by no more music. I had entered a black cloud of merciless thought, but the horse, as it chanced, worked his own way over that mountain.

"...I came down across stones dotted with pink and gray lichens....I passed a meadow and a meadow mouse in a little shower of petals struck from mountain flowers.... I rode heavily toward an old age far backward in the reptilian dark...."

I could hear the sudden ring of his hoofs as we came cautiously treading over a tilted table of granite, past the winds that blow on the high places of the world. There were stones there so polished during long ages by the storms that had rushed across them that they shone. We crossed the divide then, picking our way in places scoured by ancient ice action, through boulder fields where nothing moved and yet where one could feel time like an enemy hidden behind each stone.

If there was life on these heights, it was the thin life of mountain spiders who caught nothing in their webs, or of small gray birds that slipped soundlessly among the stones. The wind in the pass caught me head-on and blew whatever thoughts I had into a raveling stream behind me until they were all gone and there was only myself and the horse moving in an eternal dangerous present, free of the encumbrances of the past.

We crossed a wind that smelled of ice from still higher snow fields; we cantered with a breeze that came from somewhere among cedars; we passed a gust like hell's breath that had risen straight up from the desert floor. They were winds and they did not stay with us. Presently we descended out of their domain, and it was curious to see, as we dropped farther through gloomy woods and canyons, how the cleansed and scoured mind I had brought over the mountain began, like the water in those rumbling gorges, to talk in a variety of voices, to debate, to argue, to push at stones or curve subtly around obstacles. Sometimes I wonder whether we are only endlessly repeating in our heads an argument that is going on in the world's foundations among crashing stones and recalcitrant roots.

"Fall, fall, fall," cried the roaring water and the grinding pebbles in the torrent. "Let go, come with us, come home to the place without light." But the roots clung and climbed, and the trees pushed up, impeding the water, and forests filled the wind with their sighing and grasped after the sun. It is so in the mind. One can hear the rattle of falling stones in the night, and the thoughts like trees holding their place. Sometimes one can shut the noise away by turning over on the other ear; sometimes the sounds are as dreadful as a storm in the mountains, and one lies awake, holding fast like the roots that wait for daylight. It was after such a night that I came over the mountain, but it was the descent on the other side that suddenly struck me as a journey into the aeons of the past.

I came down across stones dotted with pink and gray lichens—a barren land dreaming life's last dreams in the thin air of a cold and future world.

I passed a meadow and a meadow mouse in a little shower of petals struck from mountain flowers. I dismissed it—it was almost my own time—a pleasant golden hour in the age of mammals, lost before the human coming. I rode heavily toward an old age far backward in the reptilian dark.

I was below the timber line and sinking deeper and deeper into the pine woods whose fallen needles lay thick and springy over the ungrassed slopes. The brown needles and the fallen cones, the stiff, endless green forests were a mark that placed me in the Age of Dinosaurs. I moved in silence now, waiting a sign. I saw it finally—a green lizard on a stone. We were far back, far back. He bobbed his head uncertainly at me, and I reined in with the nostalgic intent, for a moment, to call him Father; but I saw soon enough that I was a ghost who troubled him and that he would wish me, though he had not the voice to speak, to ride on. A man who comes down the road of time should not expect to converse—even with his own kin. I made a brief, uncertain sign of recognition, to which he did not respond, and passed by. Things grew more lonely. I was coming out upon the barren ridges of an old seabeach that rose along the desert floor. Life was small and grubby now. The hot, warning scarlet of peculiar desert ants occasionally flashed among the stones. I had lost all trace of myself and thought regretfully of the lizard who might have directed me.

A turned-up stone yielded only a scorpion who curled his tail in a kind of evil malice. I surveyed him reproachfully. He was old enough to know the secret of my origin, but once more an ancient, bitter animus drawn from that poisoned soil possessed him, and he raised his tail. I had been turned away. By degrees an enormous emptiness possessed me. I was back almost, in a different way, to the thin air over the mountain, to the end of all things in the cold starlight of space.

I passed some indefinable bones and shells in the salt-incrusted well of a dry arroyo. As I reined up, only sand dunes rose like waves before me; if life was there, it was no longer visible. It was like coming down to the end—to the place of fires where we began. I turned about then and let my gaze go up, tier after tier, height after height, from crawling desert bush to towering pine on the great slopes far above me.

In the same way, animal life had gone up that road from these dry, envenomed things to the deer nuzzling a fawn in the meadows far above. I had come down the whole way into a place where one could lift sand and ask in a hollow, dust-shrouded whisper, "Life, what is it? Why am I here? Why am I here?"

And my mind went up that figurative ladder of the ages, bone by bone, skull by skull, seeking an answer. There was none, except that in all that downrush of wild energy which I had passed in the canyons was this other strange organized stream that marched upward, here gaining a foothold, there tossing a pine cone a little farther upward into a crevice in the rock.

And again one asked, not of the past this time, but of the future—there where the winds howled through open space and the last lichens clung to the naked rock: "Why do we live?" There was no answer I could hear. The living river flowed out of nowhere into nothing. No one knew its source or its departing. It was an apparition. If one did not see it, there was no way to prove that it was real.

No way, that is, except within the mind itself. And the mind—in some strange manner so involved with time, moving against the cutting edge of it like the wind I had faced on the mountain—has yet its own small skull-borne replica of eternity. It is not alone that I can reach out and receive within my head a handbreadth replica of the far fields of the universe. It is not because I can touch a trilobite and know the fall of light in ages before my birth. Rather, it lies in the fact that the human mind can transcend time, even though trapped to all appearances within that medium. As from some remote place, I see myself as child and young man, watch with a certain dispassionate objectivity the violence and tears of a remote youth who was once I, shaping his character, for good or ill, toward the creature he is today. Shrinking, I see him teeter at the edge of abysses he never saw. With pain I acknowledge acts undone that might have saved and led him into some serene and noble pathway. I move about him like a ghost, that vanished youth. I exhort, I plead. He does not hear me. Indeed, he, too, is already a ghost. He has become me. I am what I am. Yet the point is, we are not wholly given over to time—if we were, such acts, such leaps through that gray medium, would be impossible. Perhaps God Himself may rove in similar pain up the dark roads of His universe. Only how would it be, I wonder, to contain at once both the beginning and the end and to hear, in helplessness perhaps, the fall of worlds in the night.

This is what the mind of man is just beginning to achieve—a little microcosm, a replica of whatever it is that from some unimaginable vantage point "outside" contains the universe and all the fractured bits of seeing which the world's creatures see. It is not necessary to ride over a mountain range to experience historical infinity. It can descend upon one in the lecture room.

"...I see it then—the trunk that stretches monstrously behind him. ...It writhes, it crawls, it barks and snuffles and roars, and the odor of the swamp exhales from it. That pale young scholar's face is the last bloom on a curious animal extrusion through time...."

It is really in daylight that the sensation I am about to describe is apt to come most clearly upon me, and for some reason, I associate it extensively with crowds. It is not, you understand, a hallucination. It is a reality. It is, I can say only with difficulty, a chink torn in a dimension that life was never intended to look through. It connotes a sense beyond the eye, although the twenty years' impressions are visual. Man, it is said, is a time-binding animal, but he was never intended for this. Here is the way it comes.

I mount the lecturer's rostrum to address a class. Like any work-worn professor fond of his subject, I fumble among my skulls and papers, shuffle to the blackboard and back again, begin the patient translation of three billion years of time into chalk scrawls and uncertain words ventured timidly to a sea of young, impatient faces. Time does not frighten them, I think enviously. They have, most of them, never lain awake and grasped the sides of a cot, staring upward into the dark while the slow clock strokes begin.

"Doctor." A voice diverts me. I stare out nearsightedly over the class. A hand from the back row gesticulates. "Doctor, do you believe there is a direction to evolution? Do you believe, Doctor. . . . Doctor, do you believe . . . ?" Instead of the words, I hear a faint piping and see an eager scholar's face squeezed and dissolving on the body of a chest-thumping ape. "Doctor, is there a direction?"

I see it then—the trunk that stretches monstrously behind him. It winds out of the door, down dark and obscure corridors to the cellar, and vanishes into the floor. It writhes, it crawls, it barks and snuffles and roars, and the odor of the swamp exhales from it. That pale young scholar's face is the last bloom on a curious animal extrusion through time. And who among us, under the cold persuasion of the archaeological eye, can perceive which of his many shapes is real or if, perhaps, the entire shape in time is not a greater and more curious animal than its single appearance.

I, too, am aware of the trunk that stretches behind me along the floor. I, too, am a many-visaged thing that has climbed upward out of the dark of endless leaf-falls and has slunk, furred, through the glitter of blue glacial nights. I, the professor, trembling absurdly on the platform with my book and spectacles, am the single philosophical animal. I am the unfolding worm and mudfish, the weird tree of Yggdrasill shaping itself endlessly out of darkness toward the light.

I have said this is not an illusion. When one sees in this manner, or when a sense of strangeness halts one on a busy street to verify the appearance of one's fellows, then one knows that a terrible new sense has opened a faint crack into the Absolute. In this way alone one comes to grips with a great mystery: that life and time bear some curious relationship to each other that is not shared by inanimate things.

It is in the brain that this world opens. To our descendants it may become a commonplace, but of me, and others like me, it has made a castaway. I have no refuge in time as others do who troop homeward at nightfall. As a result, I am one of those who linger furtively over coffee in the kitchen at bedtime or haunt the all-night restaurants. Nevertheless, I shall say without regret: there are hazards in all professions.

It may seem at this point that I have gone considerably roundabout in my examination of the natural world. I have done so in an attempt to indicate that the spider web of law, which has been flung, as Emerson indicated, across the deeps of time and space and between each member of the living world, has brought us some quite remarkable but at the same time disquieting knowledge. In rapid summary, man has passed from a natural world of appearances invisibly controlled by the caprice of spirits to an astronomical universe visualized by Newton, through the law of gravitation, as operating with the regularity of a clock.

Newton, who remained devout, assumed that God, at the time of the creation of the solar system, had set everything to operating in its proper orbit. He recognized, however, certain irregularities of planetary movement which, in time, would lead to a disruption of his perfect astronomical machine. It was here, as a seventeenth-century scholar, that he felt no objection to the notion that God interfered at periodical intervals to correct the deviations of the machine.

A century later Laplace had succeeded in dispensing with this last vestige of divine intervention. The eighteenth-century geologist James Hutton had similarly dealt with supernaturalism in earth-building, and Darwin, in the nineteenth century, had gone far toward producing a similar mechanistic explanation of life. The machine that began in the heavens had finally been installed in the human heart and brain. "We can make everything natural," Pascal had truly said, and surely the more naïve forms of worship of the unseen are vanishing.

"...If all life were to be swept from the world, leaving only its chemical constituents, no visitor from another star would be able to establish the reality of such a phantom...."

Yet strangely, with the discovery of evolutionary, as opposed to purely durational time, there emerges into this safe and sane mechanical universe something quite unanticipated by the eighteenth-century rationalists—a kind of emergent, if not miraculous, novelty.

I know that the word "miraculous" is regarded dubiously in scientific circles because of past quarrels with theologians. The word has been defined, however, as an event transcending the known laws of nature. Since, as we have seen, the laws of nature have a way of being altered from one generation of scientists to the next, a little taste for the miraculous in this broad sense will do us no harm. We forget that Nature herself is one vast miracle transcending the reality of night and nothingness. We forget that each one of us in his personal life repeats that miracle.

Whatever may be the power behind those dancing sparks to which the physicist has penetrated, it makes the light of the muskrat's world as it makes the world of the great poet. It makes, in fact, all of the innumerable and private worlds that exist in the head of man. There is a sense in which we can say that the planet, with its strange freight of life, is always just passing from the unnatural to the natural, from that Unseen which man has always reverenced to the small reality of the day. If all life were to be swept from the world, leaving only its chemical constituents, no visitor from another star would be able to establish the reality of such a phantom. The dust would lie without visible protest, as it does now in the moon's airless craters or in the road before our door.

Yet this is the same dust which, dead, quiescent, and unmoving, when taken up in the process known as life, hears music and responds to it, weeps bitterly over time and loss, or is oppressed by the looming future that is, in any materialist terms, the veriest shadow of nothing. How natural was man, we may ask, until he came? What forces dictated that a walking ape should watch the red shift of light beyond the island universe or listen by carefully devised antennae to the pulse of unseen stars? Who, whimsically, conceived that the plot of the world should begin in a mud puddle and end where, and with whom? Men argue learnedly over whether life is chemical chance or anti-chance, but they seem to forget that the life *in* chemicals may be the greatest chance of all, the most mysterious and inexplicable property in matter.

"The special value of science," a perceptive philosopher once wrote, "lies not in what it makes of the world, but in what it makes of the knower." Some years ago, while camping in a vast eroded area in the West, I came upon one of those unlikely sights which illuminate such truths.

I suppose that nothing living had moved among those great stones for centuries. They lay toppled against one another like fallen dolmens. The huge stones were beasts, I used to think, of a sort man ordinarily lived too fast to understand. They seemed inanimate because the tempo of the life in them was slow. They lived ages in one place and only moved when man was not looking. Sometimes at night I would hear a low rumble as one drew itself into a new position and subsided again. Sometimes I found their tracks ground deeply into the hillsides.

It was with considerable surprise, therefore, that while traversing this barren valley, I came, one afternoon, upon what I can only describe as a remarkable sight. Some distance away, so far that for a little space I could make nothing of the spectacle, my eyes were attracted by a dun-colored object, about the size of a football, that periodically bounded up from the desert floor. Wonderingly, I drew closer and observed that something ropelike, which glittered in the sun, appeared to be dangling from the ball-shaped object. Whatever the object was, it appeared to be bouncing faster and more desperately as I approached. My surroundings were such that this hysterical dance of what at first glance appeared to be a common stone was quite unnerving, as though suddenly all the natural objects in the valley were about to break into a jig. Going closer, I penetrated the mystery.

The sun was sparkling on the scales of a huge blacksnake that was partially looped about the body of a hen pheasant. Desperately the bird tried to rise, and just as desperately the big snake coiled and clung, though each time the bird, falling several feet, pounded the snake's body in the gravel. I gazed at the scene in astonishment. Here in this silent waste, like an emanation from nowhere, two bitter and desperate vapors, two little whirlwinds of contending energy, were beating each other to death because of their plans—something, I suspected, about whether a clutch of eggs was to turn into a thing with wings or scales—this problem of the onrushing, non-existent future had catapulted serpent against bird.

The bird was too big for the snake to have had it in mind as prey. Most probably the snake had been intent on stealing the pheasant's eggs and had been set upon and pecked. Somehow in the ensuing scuffle he had flung a loop over the bird's back and partially blocked her wings. The bird could not take off, and the snake would not let go. The snake was taking a heavy battering on the stones, but the high-speed metabolism and tremendous flight-exertion of the mother bird were rapidly exhausting her. I stood for a moment and saw the bloodshot glaze deepen in her eyes. I suppose I could have waited there to see what would happen when she could not fly; I suppose it might have been worth recording for science. But I could not stand that ceaseless, bloody pounding in the gravel. I thought of the eggs somewhere about, and wondered whether they were to elongate and writhe into an armor of scales or eventually to go whistling into the wind with their wild mother.

So I, the mammal, in my way supple and less bound by instinct, arbitrated the matter. I unwound the serpent from the bird and let him hiss and wrap his battered coils around my arm. The bird, her wings flung out, rocked on her legs and gasped repeatedly. I moved away in order not to drive her farther from her nest. Thus the serpent and I, two terrible and feared beings, passed quickly out of view.

Over the next ridge, where he could do no more damage, I let the snake, whose anger had subsided, slowly uncoil and slither from my arm. He flowed away into a little patch of bunch grass—aloof, forgetting, unaware of the journey he had made upon my wrist, which throbbed from his expert constriction. The bird had contended for birds against the oncoming future; the serpent writhing into the bunch grass had contended just as desperately for serpents. And I, the apparition in that valley—for what had I contended, I who contained the serpent and the bird and who read the past long written in their bodies?

As I sauntered dwarfed among overhanging pinnacles, as the great slabs which were the visible remnants of past ages lay their enormous shadows rhythmically as life and death across my face, slowly the answer came to me: man could contain more than himself. Among these many appearances that flew, or swam in waters, or wavered momentarily into being, he alone possessed that unique ability.

The Renaissance thinkers were right when they said that man, the microcosm, contains the macrocosm. I had touched the lives of creatures other than myself and had seen their shapes waver and blow like smoke through the corridors of time. With sudden concentrated attention, I had watched myself, this brain, unrolling from the seed like a genie from a bottle, and, casting my eyes forward, I had seen it vanish again into the formless alchemies of the earth.

For what, then, had I contended, weighing the serpent with the bird in that wild valley? I had struggled, I am now convinced, for a greater, more comprehensive version of myself.

"...I am a man who has spent a great deal of his life on his knees, though not in prayer....I am a naturalist and a fossil hunter, and I have crawled most of the way through life....In man, I know now, there is no such thing as wisdom...."

I am a man who has spent a great deal of his life on his knees, though not in prayer. I do not say this last pridefully, but with the feeling that the posture, if not the thought behind it, may have had some final salutary effect. I am a naturalist and a fossil hunter, and I have crawled most of the way through life. I have crawled downward into holes without bottom, and upward into crevices where the wind and the birds screamed at me until the sound of a falling pebble was enough to make the sick heart lurch. In man, I know now, there is no such thing as wisdom. I have learned this with my face against the ground. It is a very difficult thing for a man to grasp today, because of his power; yet in his brain there is really only a sort of universal marsh, spotted at intervals by quaking green islands representing the elusive stability of modern science—islands frequently gone as soon as glimpsed.

It is our custom to deny this; we are men of precision, measurement, and logic; we abhor the unexplainable and reject it. This, too, is a green island. We wish our lives to be one continuous growth in knowledge; indeed, we expect them to be. Yet well over a hundred years ago, a great theologian,

Kierkegaard, observed that maturity consists in the discovery that "there comes a critical moment where everything is reversed, after which the point becomes to understand more and more that there is something which cannot be understood."

When I separated the serpent from the bird and released them in that wild upland, it was not for knowledge, not for anything I had learned in science. Instead, I contained, to put it simply, the serpent and the bird. I would always contain them. I was no longer one of the contending vapors; I had embraced them in my own substance and, in some insubstantial way, reconciled them as I had sought reconciliation with the muskrat on the shore. I had transcended feather and scale and gone beyond them into another sphere of reality. I was trying to give birth to a different self whose only expression lies again in the deeply religious words of Pascal: "You would not seek me had you not found me."

I had not known what I sought, but I was aware at last that something had found me. I no longer believed that nature was either natural or unnatural, only that nature now appears natural to man. But the nature that appears natural to man is another version of the muskrat's world under the boat dock and the elusive sparks over which the physicist made his trembling passage. They were appearances, specialized insights, but unreal because in the constantly onrushing future they were swept away.

What had become of the natural world of that gorilla-headed little ape from which we sprang—that dim, African corner with its chewed fishbones and giant Ice Age pigs? It was gone more utterly than my muskrat's tiny domain; yet it had given birth to an unimaginable thing—ourselves—something overreaching the observable laws of that far epoch. Man since the beginning seems to be awaiting an event, the nature of which he does not know. "With reference to the near past," Thoreau once shrewdly observed, "we all occupy the region of common sense, but in the prospect of the future we are, by instinct, transcendentalists." This is the way of the man who makes nature "natural." He stands at the point where the miraculous comes into being, and after the event he calls it "natural." The imagination of man, in its highest manifestations, stands close to the doorway of the infinite, to the world beyond the nature that we know. Perhaps, after all, in this respect, man constitutes the exertion of that act which Donne three centuries ago called God's prerogative.

Man's quest for certainty is, in the last analysis, a quest for meaning. But the meaning lies buried within himself rather than in the void that he has vainly searched for portents since antiquity. Perhaps the first act in its unfolding was taken by a raw beast with a fearsome head who dreamed some difficult and unimaginable thing denied his fellows. Perhaps the flashes of beauty and insight which trouble us so deeply are no less prophetic of what the race might achieve. All that prevents us is doubt—the power to make everything natural without the accompanying gift to see, beyond the natural, to that inexpressible realm in which the words "natural" and "supernatural" cease to have meaning.

Man, at last, is face to face with himself in natural guise. "What we make natural, we destroy," said Pascal. He knew, with superlative insight, man's complete necessity to transcend the worldly image that this word connotes. It is not the outward powers of Man the Toolmaker that threaten us. It is a growing danger which has already afflicted vast areas of the world—the danger that we have created an unbearable last idol for our worship. That idol, that uncreated and ruined visage which confronts us daily, is no less than man made natural. Beyond this replica of ourselves, this countenance already grown so distantly inhuman that it terrifies us, still beckons the lonely figure of men's dreams. It is a nature, not of this age, but of the becoming—the light once glimpsed by a creature just over the threshold from a beast, a despairing cry from the dark shadow of a cross on Golgotha long ago.

Man is not totally compounded of the nature we profess to understand. Man is always partly of the future, which he possesses a power to shape. "Natural" is a magician's word—and like all such, it should be used sparingly lest there arise from it, as now, some unglimpsed, unintended world, some monstrous caricature called into being by the indiscreet articulation of worn syllables. Perhaps, if we are wise, we will prefer to stand like those humble creatures who poured little gifts of flints into a grave. Perhaps there may come to us then, in some such moment, a ghostly sense that an invisible doorway has been opened—a doorway which, widening out, will take man beyond the nature that he knows.

THE
BAROQUE
AGE

KAREL PLICKA, PRAGUE

INGE MORATH—MAGNUM

The Baroque Age

Grandiose, sensual, mystical, always turbulent, it produced an art as adventurous as its life

By CARL J. FRIEDRICH

"The architecture of the Baroque speaks the same language as that of the Renaissance, but a brutalized version of it." So wrote the great Swiss art historian Jacob Burckhardt just over a century ago. The idea spread and persisted for many a year that not only in architecture but in all the arts the Baroque was little more than an ugly, perverted, overdone excrescence of the Renaissance. This is still the judgment of many who have a reasonably clear notion of the Gothic and the Renaissance itself, along with the Classic and the Romantic, but for whom the Baroque remains a confused, uncertain concept.

Much nearer our own time, however, the historian Oswald Spengler went to an opposite extreme in speaking of the Baroque. The gigantic, if wrong-headed, portrait of Western man and his civilization that Spengler painted a generation ago celebrated the Baroque age as the high point of our culture; ever since that time, he thought, the decline of the West had progressed rapidly.

Between such opposing views, a middle ground of new interest in the nature and scope of the Baroque has spread. Today, no past period is the subject of so much debate and, perhaps, of so much curiosity. Men of our time have developed a better grasp than the classicist Burckhardt ever had of a period that embraced Bernini and Rembrandt, Descartes and Spinoza, Milton and Bach. A sense of kinship is felt with it today, not only in the fine arts but in poetry and music as well. Contemporary composers find more inspiration there than in works from later periods, and the same holds for poets and dramatists, even for philosophers. Many critics now recognize and celebrate the Baroque as a great and distinct age, although not necessarily calling it the highest point of our culture as Spengler did.

A Baroque love of curves, movement, and illusion (embodied in a trompe-l'œil *ceiling) enriches the Clementinum Library (opposite) in Prague's Jesuit college, begun before 1600.*

How shall we define and delimit the Baroque? Its beginnings reach far back into the sixteenth century, but its first great manifestations appear in the last quarter of it. The seventeenth century is, however, its true domain, with further extensions (especially in music, often a late arrival) far into the eighteenth. Styles are like mountain peaks merging into each other in the valleys between; the peak of the Baroque ought perhaps to be placed around the year 1650.

Like all styles, it has no uniform set of traits, but can be better described by an analogy to two magnetic poles operating within a common field of ideas and feelings. This common field was focused on movement, intensity, tension, force. As contrasted with the debonair worldliness of the Renaissance, reflected in the luminous harmony of the paintings of Raphael, the Baroque was tormented by doubts, shot through with conflicts and extremes. Not a happy and unreflective pleasure of the senses, but gross sensuality alternating with pangs of conscience becomes the dominant note. The Baroque age was torn between extremes. The warm-blooded *Sinnenfreude* of the previous age turned into coarse materialism and carnal debauch, while the philosophical and scholarly inquiries of humanism led to skepticism and scientific discovery.

Tension and intensity are natural to music and, to some extent, to painting, but they produce seemingly insoluble problems for the static arts of architecture and sculpture. The word "Baroque" suggests the grotesque, the overladen, the extravagant. Baroque is all that. But it has a beauty of its own which is missed when viewed from the canons of classical aesthetics. Such canons had ruled supreme during the Renaissance. But by 1600 they were dead. Painting, sculpture, and music had exhausted the possibilities of that approach. Something new was needed.

Why was it needed? What overpowering drive gives a new style its meaning and significance? This is and remains a mystery. We cannot penetrate the inner sanctum of the creative impulse, but we may enter into the courtyard. Here we find new experiences which shape the feeling and thinking of men as they enter upon a new age. The style that results is the outward projection of such new experiences around one central, shattering explosion. In the age that ushered in the Baroque, the explosion was partly cosmic and partly social. Cosmically, it was an experience begot by the Copernican discovery that the earth is not the center of the universe, but only a fragment of it, and not a particularly significant one at that. The comfortable notion of man in the middle of an earth-centered universe gave way to the lonely vision of man lost in the vastnesses of infinite space. But this discovery was accompanied by a sense of incredible new power born of the same new science—the power to see what is very far away, and the even more startling power to interpret the harmony of the spheres as an order obeying laws which man can know and manipulate to extend his dominion over nature.

To this exciting experience of power reaching into the infinite, beyond all dreams of former ages, was added another in the world of politics. The modern state was emerging from the chaos of the religious wars of the sixteenth century and supplanting the feudal order which had disintegrated. With its central bureaucracy and standing army or navy, this modern state was indeed a new order. As it organized and directed ever larger masses of men, and encircled the globe in the empires of Spain, France,

The new age agreed with Shakespeare: "All the world's a stage." Peter Paul Rubens mirrored the expansive theater of Baroque taste when in his allegorical The Education of Marie de Medici, *c. 1622 (opposite), he portrayed the future French queen before a backdrop fountain on Mount Parnassus, learning the arts of music, literature, and eloquence from Apollo, Athena, and Hermes, respectively, while the Three Graces stand by to offer her beauty and allure. A favorite symbol was the tortuous mourning angel, such as Bernini's on Rome's Ponte Sant'Angelo (above).*

and Britain, the new state again embodied power of a magnitude never before experienced. The close-knit community of the town behind its walls crumbled, along with the independence of the nobility in their castles. And once again, as the ancient bulwarks of local pride and power sank into ruins, there was also a sense of utter helplessness in the face of such new might. Here, too, man was seized by a novel feeling of loneliness, of isolation and despair.

Some great styles are characterized by a profound polarity—an inner contradiction that springs from the experience upon which they are built. These are the styles of "open" form—the Gothic, the Romantic, as well as the Baroque. The experience of power on one hand and of utter lack of it on the other, of potency and impotence, was at the core of man's new attitude to the world around him. Artists and writers, musicians and philosophers sought to express it. Was there ever a more power-haunted face than the portrait Frans Hals painted of René Descartes? Was ever a more dramatic paean sung to power than the challenge Satan issues to God in Milton's *Paradise Lost?* One philosopher whose life spans the Baroque age as if he were to be its symbol is Thomas Hobbes. Born in 1588, not long after the completion of the pioneer Baroque church of Il Gesù in Rome (see illustration on page 52), he lived until 1679, brooding over man's life as "a restless desire for power after power that ceases only in death."

But the drama of power and of man's despair in striving for power is not the complete story. It is merely the Baroque's vital center. Around it are grouped the fantastic possibilities which artists, scientists, and men of politics discovered when "attempting the impossible." This fascination with power and the despair over man's impotence created Baroque man's deep concern with death and the dreamlike quality of life. Shakespeare, in the Baroque mood of his late work *The Tempest,* calls the world a stage, as does the utterly Baroque Spaniard, Calderón. So strong was the era's feeling for the delusive, theatrical nature of man's existence that the great men of the age had themselves portrayed as players of dramatic roles. The large paintings of Richelieu by Champaigne and of Olivares by Velázquez (see pages 40 and 41) testify to this sense of ever-present drama. It is no wonder that the wig was in fashion in the seventeenth century. Although originally merely a device for hiding Louis XIII's baldness, the wig spread very fast among people who saw themselves as actors in the *Theatrum Mundi*—the title of a seventeenth-century Who's Who and Encyclopedia rolled into one.

There was, however, one escape from the tension between power and despair. The Baroque age shares with the Gothic age the distinction of having produced Christianity's deepest mystics. In Spain, in France, in Germany, in England, everywhere, people confronted with the finite in man and the infinity of spirit and cosmos sought refuge in relinquishing completely the cares of this world. Saint Theresa and John of the Cross in Spain, François de Sales and Pascal in France, Angelus Silesius and Jakob Boehme in Germany, John Donne, Sir Thomas Browne, and John Bunyan in England—these are only the most remarkable among a host of spiritual thinkers and doers. The mysterious figure of Richelieu's *"éminence grise,"* Père Joseph, a mystic and yet a devoted servant of the ruthless struggle for power, was the very Baroque link between the two worlds of the mystic and the statesman.

Two symbolic figures recur in Baroque literature and court ballet: the peacock and Circe. The peacock is the traditional symbol of vanity and display; Circe, of course, is the beautiful enchantress who transformed Ulysses' companions into pigs. The strutting and play-acting of Baroque man is peacocklike indeed. The way of the women who lend color to the seventeenth century is feminine in the old-fashioned sense: charming, deceitful, intriguing—and certainly capable of turning men into pigs. The great ladies of France, from the Queen to the fabulous Duchesse de Chevreuse, spun their plots, played with men and kingdoms. To this day, the parks of the great castles which the Baroque age has left us are appropriately inhabited by stately, preening peacocks. Circe and the peacock figuratively greet us as we enter the Piazza Navona in Rome—one of the high points of Baroque art (see illustration, page 51), with its fountains by Bernini and the façade of the church of Sant' Agnese by Borromini—and beckon us to delve more deeply into the elated and yet tormented souls that erected these masterworks.

There was a time when, stimulated by the Swiss-German art historian Heinrich Wölfflin, it was the fashion to assert that the Baroque was the radical opposite of the Renaissance. Such a view grew out of seeing the Baroque style as a corrupted Renaissance style. Styles rarely stand in such antithesis to each other. They evolve naturally out of each other and bear close resemblance, particularly in periods of transition. It is easy to describe the stylistic difference between Raphael and Rembrandt; it is not so easy in the case of Correggio and Caravaggio. Raphael (see page 44) has clear, contrasting colors and linear, sharply defined outlines presenting separate and distinct figures or objects in harmonious relation, whereas Rembrandt, especially in his late period, paints in chiaroscuro; thus browns, grays, and black, contrasted with yellow, predominate, the outlines merge with the background, and typically either *one* figure or a mass of figures composes one scene. To heighten contrast, Rembrandt very often lets the light fall upon the focal point of interest (page 47), while Raphael's pictures are so fully "in the light" that the beholder is not conscious of a source of light at all.

But in any case, we cannot say of stylistic periods that one begins where the other ends. While the builders of Il Gesù were working, in the decade around 1575, on their novel design of what was to be the first Baroque church,

TEXT CONTINUED ON PAGE 42

POPE URBAN VIII

JOHANNES KEPLER

CLAUDIO MONTEVERDI

RENE DESCARTES

BLAISE PASCAL

THOMAS HOBBES

PIERRE CORNEILLE

JOHN MILTON

KING GUSTAVUS ADOLPHUS

The faces of Baroque men tell of their era's variety, vigor, and intensity. These nine were only some of the age's movers and shakers who broke new ground in every field of art and thought. All were daring spirits, all innovators: from left to right, tier by tier above, they include a Counter Reformation pope who wrote poems and hymns and commissioned great buildings, a German astronomer who discovered laws of planetary motion, an Italian pioneer composer of opera; a great French rationalist thinker, a Jansenist pietist and mathematician, and an English philosopher of statecraft; a classical French playwright, the English Puritan who composed the soaring Baroque epic Paradise Lost, *and an inspired Swedish warrior-king.*

While surging discoveries and enthusiasms inspired the new age, savage religious and national struggles darkened it. Among its great actors were mighty ministers of state dedicated to advancing their rival dynasties and themselves. France's weak Louis XIII was brilliantly served by the supple Cardinal Richelieu (above, in a portrait by Philippe de Champaigne): Spain's Philip IV, less well by the flamboyant Count-Duke of Olivares (right, as painted in the 1630's by Velázquez). Although staunch fellow Catholics in a continent beset by English and Huguenot rise, the two ministers were bitter antagonists, and Richelieu's Paris machinations served, prophetically, to reduce the power of the Austro-Spanish House of Hapsburg.

TEXT CONTINUED FROM PAGE 38

much building in clear Renaissance style was going on all around them, and the great Palladio was flourishing as the last crowning glory of Renaissance architecture. The story of the Baroque, as of all styles, is the history of its spread from a center, in successive waves that produced new and distinctive national and regional variations. Rome and Italy were for the Baroque what the Ile-de-France was for the Gothic, the heart and inspiration of a style that helped to shape all art and life throughout Europe to the end of the seventeenth century.

What, then, are the characteristic features of the Baroque style? Like all styles, it has no simple, single trait by which it can be characterized, but rather a cluster of them, grouped around antithetical poles. Like the experience of power from which it sprang, Baroque art is limitless; its protagonists attempt the "impossible." In their concentration on movement and force, they were great experimenters with untried forms and materials. Many interpreters have stressed the Baroque artists' preoccupation with time, as against space alone. It has been said that they gave even spatial relationships a temporal dimension. You can walk into Baroque paintings: they draw you into their landscapes with the distant views, the misty horizons, and setting suns beloved by Claude Lorrain (page 47), one of the greatest Baroque painters. It is the infinite which these horizons hint at; Claude, who at the same time was preoccupied with light, somehow succeeded in painting time. Of him, Goethe could say to Eckermann: "There is not a trace of reality in his pictures, but the highest truth. . . ."

METROPOLITAN MUSEUM OF ART, DICK FUND 1924

A censer exudes Baroque aroma

In Baroque poetry, too, a sense of the passage of time and of the inexorable destruction it brings is very prominent. It dominates the work of such poets and writers as Góngora, Lope de Vega, and Calderón, the mature Shakespeare, Donne and Milton, Corneille, Grimmelshausen, and others too numerous to mention.

Was it an accident that a great American writer of our time should choose Donne's immortal words about the tolling of the bell as the title of one of his most moving novels? (The passage from which they were taken appears on page 58.) The symbol of the bell speaks of the passage of time, and of the death that comes to all. Indeed, in Donne's prose and poetry almost all the great themes of Baroque writing—from fleshly lust to the most mystic metaphysics—are intoned. Of Donne it has been said that he was "more medieval and more modern than the Renaissance." That is to say, he was Baroque. For, in a sense, the Baroque is the impossible effort to unite the spirit of the Gothic with that of the Renaissance in a new synthesis.

This concern with time and death caused the preoccupation with such symbols as the skull and the skeleton. "The men of the Baroque differed from those of other epochs . . . they liked an art that harps on death and corruption," Aldous Huxley has remarked. Yet at the same time they liked an art that was also sensual and profoundly worldly, such as that of Rubens. Baroque artists and writers were forever going to the extreme while probing the depth of human emotion.

But we are still speaking of *what* they did. Which forms did the Baroque favor?

Baroque art found its richest fulfillment, it seems to me, in the opera. It was this age which invented the form, Claudio Monteverdi's *Orfeo* (1607) having been called the first opera—although *Euridice* by Peri and Caccini predated it by seven years. *Orfeo* was followed by many others, among which Monteverdi's *The Coronation of Poppea* (1642) is outstanding. Written in the monodic style, they are markedly different from what we today think of as opera, as embodied in the work of Mozart, Verdi, and Wagner. But the opera remains at its outset a Baroque creation, blending many different arts into a harmonious whole—architecture with painting, sculpture, poetry, and music, not to speak of acting and the *grande toilette* of the ladies attending. The many pictures we have of great opera performances (see pages 61 and 63) are rivaled by dramatic descriptions which fill today's reader with nostalgia as he realizes that he can never hope really to relive the world of the Baroque in all its sumptuous, if fleeting, pomp and splendor.

That such a style should have given rise to much that was ugly and even horrible goes without saying. In trying to break all bounds and accomplish the impossible, the Baroque artist often achieved merely the ludicrous. This is particularly evident in certain extravaganzas of church architecture, in the gilded interiors of chateaux which were bad copies of Versailles, and in the more fearsome elaborations of Baroque poetry, especially in Italy. It is therefore rather easy to recite bad verses or to portray bad architecture as typical of the Baroque, and to forget the magnificent procession of superb achievements which the age produced.

In architecture, it brought forth the richly ornamented façade, the sweep of flowing staircases, the ornamental garden opening out toward a distant view. Reflect for a moment upon the staircase. The Renaissance sought to hide it, as did Jefferson with his classicist leanings. For the staircase suggests movement and, in doing so, portrays the flux

TEXT CONTINUED ON PAGE 50

AN UPHEAVAL IN PAINTING

COURTESY THE DOWAGER LADY ABERCONWAY

Many of the greatest Baroque artists (Rubens, Rembrandt, and Claude Lorrain, for instance) died long before the term "Baroque" was born. Coined by eighteenth-century classicists, it was first intended to denote with disdain the irregular, extravagant, disorderly, bizarre. Yet later generations have found more qualities than these in the masters who rebelled against Renaissance ideals of order, harmony, and timeless grace in a pursuit of passion, conflict, and intensely personal vision. The paintings on this and the following pages suggest the range and force of their explosion—none more so than The Temple of Janus *(above) by the Venetian Sebastiano Mazzoni (1611–1678), an artist long forgotten and rediscovered only in our own day.*

RAPHAEL: CRUCIFIXION, C. 1500

The new era's revolution in art is exemplified by two paintings of the same subject by masters working 120 years apart. Raphael's Crucifixion *(left) was painted about 1500, at the stately peak of the High Renaissance; Rubens's version (right), shortly after the outbreak of the Thirty Years' War, when new fervor and violence coupled with Baroque sensibility were sweeping the continent of Europe.*

Raphael records the great act of redemption with restraint, dignity, monumentality. Here is no frenzied moment, but time suspended in a seemingly eternal scene. Landscape and figures are bathed in a clear, pervasive light, subtly modeled without strong shadows. Every outline is distinct, each color painted for its own sake; the figures stand in relief against the background. Rubens, in contrast, boldly catches the moment in which the centurion strikes his lance. The calm balance of the Renaissance is abandoned for the expression of passionate tension suggesting time, motion, dynamic power. While Raphael arranges his figures symmetrically, in the pyramidal composition favored in his age, Rubens chooses the dramatic diagonal composition beloved of the Baroque. He softens contours against a swirling background of color; he manipulates the light to model his figures powerfully and to cast shadows portentous of the divine tragedy that is his subject. The brilliant distinctiveness that marks each of Raphael's figures is subordinated in Rubens to a tumultuous whole. His thieves writhe, and Mary Magdalen raises her arms against the lance. All is thrust and counterthrust. If Raphael's goal is to have the spectator contemplate spiritual beauty, Rubens's is to seize and enlist the emotions.

ROYAL MUSEUM OF FINE ARTS, ANTWERP

Peter Paul Rubens: Crucifixion Altar, 1620

COURTESY TRUSTEES OF THE NATIONAL GALLERY, LONDON

Francisco Zurbarán:
St. Francis Kneeling, c. 1639

CHURCH OF SANTA MARIA DEL POPOLO, ROME

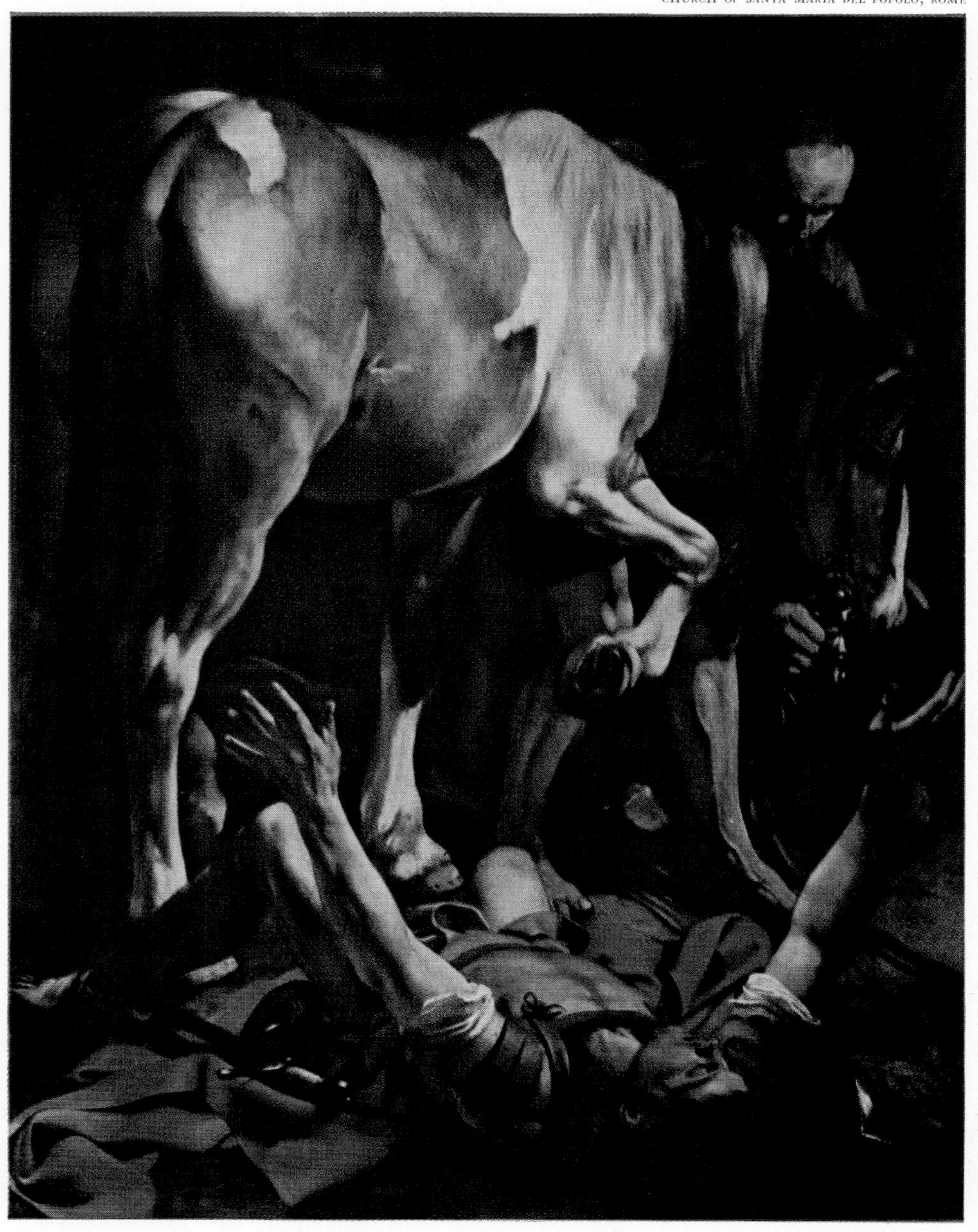

Michelangelo da Caravaggio: The Conversion of St. Paul, c. 1600

Boundless in its assertion of energy, emotion, and individuality, the Baroque spirit encouraged artists to strike out in many directions on their own. The four painters represented here were far removed from one another in place, language, and style; yet all were linked by adventurousness. A more specific bond was their common attachment to realism: both in the Catholic southern countries and in Rembrandt's Protestant north, the new gospel was to "imitate natural things well." Not that Baroque painters forswore the allegorical and religious subject matter of the Renaissance, but they did take fresh interest in landscape, atmosphere, still life. Caravaggio in his time was assailed for the realism of such canvases as The Conversion of St. Paul *(left), while the Spanish mysticism of Zurburán (above) and the Lutheran piety of Rembrandt (opposite, below) startled many with their psychological depth and religious fervor. Meanwhile, the Frenchman Claude Lorrain explored endless space in harbor scenes such as his* Embarcation *(opposite, above). All these painters were interested in light and what it could reveal of drama, mystery, and space. All were also deeply concerned with the human soul.*

BY COURTESY OF THE TRUSTEES OF THE NATIONAL GALLERY, LONDON

CLAUDE LORRAIN: EMBARCATION OF THE QUEEN OF SHEBA, 1648

BULLOZ–MUSEE JACQUEMART-ANDRE, PARIS

REMBRANDT: THE SUPPER AT EMMAUS, 1629

OVERLEAF: A peak of monumental Baroque painting was reached in Fra Andrea Pozzo's ceiling fresco for the nave of Sant' Ignazio in Rome. This allegory of Jesuit missionary work, done in 1691–1694, is both the ultimate in the depiction of mystic glory and the epitome of illusionist invention. In the photograph on the following pages, the windows and the lowest arches at either end are real; all else, including the columns and upper arches, is painted on a vaulted ceiling whose curve follows that of the arch at lower left. Pozzo's virtuosity with perspective seems to open the roof for an ascent into a glorious heaven.

OVERLEAF PHOTOGRAPH BY ANDERSON

EVROPA
ASIA

TEXT CONTINUED FROM PAGE 42

of time. This dramatic feature of the staircase endeared it to Baroque architects who, without question, created the most beautiful staircases of the Western world, which nothing before or since can rival. As for façades and dramatic detail, there is such a wealth of Baroque marvels that one can hardly choose, but Saint Peter's Colonnade in Rome (page 52), Versailles and its many rivals, more especially the Bishop's Palace at Würzburg and the cloister churches of Wies, Vierzehnheiligen, and Melk (page 55), and finally, Saint Paul's at London are among the most outstanding. The names of the great architects of this era range from Bernini and Borromini through Mansart to Balthasar Neumann and Wren. To them one is tempted to add Michelangelo, the man who in some of his most remarkable work, like the Sistine Chapel, seems to transcend the Renaissance and herald the coming stylistic revolution.

In painting, the same dramatic preoccupation can be seen. Hard outlines and sharp color contrasts yield to the merging of object and background in chiaroscuro, and instead of the primary colors, the many-hued browns, grays, and greens become predominant in most Baroque masters, especially Rembrandt, Champaigne, and Claude Lorrain. There are Baroque painters, such as Rubens, Poussin, and Velázquez, who only occasionally display the twilight shades; they achieve similar infinitudes by massive movement and dramatic posture as well as by the distant perspective. In the great landscape painters of the Low Countries, from Rubens to Ruysdael, the sky often becomes predominant. Again and again one feels the wind blowing, one is chilled by the fast-drifting clouds. In not a few paintings, a storm is raging: a drama of destruction that conveys the feeling of the passage of time. Torn and uprooted trees, abandoned ruins, and the driftwood of the seashore touch the same chord. And yet it is equally Baroque to descend to the common depth, to the lusty peasant, drinking and making merry, as portrayed by Teniers, or more gently by the Brothers Le Nain.

Closely connected with this sense of time and movement is the preoccupation with individuality in man and nature. Portraiture had been a key concern of the Occident for several centuries, but the earlier faces have a timeless quality of eternal youth or manhood. Baroque art produced its greatest masterworks in the portrayal of the old and the very young: Velázquez's children and Rembrandt's old men and women represent the pinnacle of this new way of seeing the human being in its temporal setting, where the now and here is merely a parable of what has been and is yet to come.

Theater and the drama, more especially the heroic tragedy, really came into their own during the Baroque period. Whether or not we should we call Shakespeare "Baroque" may be argued, but the structure of his plays, bursting the bounds of established canons, is stylistically in line with Baroque conceptions; and in dramas like *King Lear* (1609), he surely attempts the "impossible" in the portrayal of human emotions. In any case, recent scholarship inclines to claim at least the Shakespeare of after 1606 for the Baroque—and certainly Lope de Vega, Calderón, and the host of other Spanish dramatists of the generations after 1570 are Baroque to the core. They in turn inspired Corneille, who in many ways founded the French theater. He was followed by Racine and Molière, and finally by Lully, the man who transformed Italian opera into something very French, even though he himself was an Italian.

French historians of literature and culture have only recently begun to acknowledge the intensely Baroque quality of their great classicists. Even now, the conventional view is that French classicism is something special unto itself, not only in literature but in architecture as well. And indeed it is. It is the French version of the Baroque. But classicism, rightly understood, is not a style, but a particular way of treating any style. Goethe, the classicist, was a leading figure of the Romantic age. Unquestionably, some styles, like that of the Renaissance, have a particular affinity with the worked-out rules of Greek art. But that is all. Let us take *Le Cid* of Corneille. It is a drama of honor, not only of Spanish honor but of French and universal honor; all other values must be sacrified to this highest good. It challenges even the most sacred taboo of the age, the authority of the monarch. Against the appeal of the courtier that he should submit to the king's will, the Count asserts:

"Et l'on peut me réduire à vivre sans bonheur
Mais non pas me résoudre de vivre sans honneur."

Throughout this drama, written in rigid Alexandrine verse, there pulses an all-engulfing passion. The work displays the unique power of formalized representation of the emotions. To a later age such scenes as those between the two lovers in *Le Cid* seem stilted and stagy, as indeed they are compared with Shakespeare's. But this view fails to appreciate the cult of form, which achieved its greatest triumphs in the classicist versions of the Baroque.

Yet form dissolves amid the favorite theme of life's illusion. It appears frequently in Shakespeare, but perhaps the most perfect Baroque creation embodying it is Calderón's *La Vida Es Sueño* (*Life Is a Dream*). Here we find the parallel to Hamlet's "To be or not to be": *"Que toda*

TEXT CONTINUED ON PAGE 64

A Baroque key

A FESTIVE ARCHITECTURE

ROBERT EMMETT BRIGHT–RAPHO-GUILLUMETTE

Breaking free from Renaissance restraints, Baroque builders delighted in the exuberant façade, the dramatic vista, the busy perspective, and sought to unite architecture, decoration, and city planning in that greatest of outdoor show places, the square. In Rome's Piazza Navona (above), Gianlorenzo Bernini produced such an integrated masterwork. Using the site of the ancient circus of Domitian and its surviving obelisk, he designed a festive space with three fountains (in the foreground, the Fontana del Moro), so grouped that Borromini's prodigious Baroque church of Sant'Agnese (left), built soon after under Pope Innocent X's patronage, become their focus.

JOHN B. VINCENT

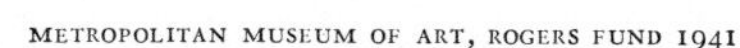

METROPOLITAN MUSEUM OF ART, ROGERS FUND 1941

When the young Jesuit order projected a mother church that would hold its growing congregation in Rome and embody the new spirit of the Counter Reformation, architects Giacomo della Porta and Giacomo da Vignola achieved by 1584 the pace-setting Il Gesù (upper left). Wide and massive, it retained classical elements but heralded a new style with its powerful lateral scrolls. From there the Baroque ecclesiastical manner rose rapidly to heights of the brilliant and spectacular. In the 1660's, Bernini's immense colonnades ennobled the piazza of St. Peter's (below, left, in an etching by Piranesi), their author remarking of them that they symbolized two mighty, motherly arms that would "embrace Catholics to reinforce their belief, heretics to reunite them with the Church, and agnostics to enlighten them with the true faith." In Vienna, half a century later, Fischer von Erlach, one of the most theatrical of Baroque builders, designed the extravagant Karlskirche (right), with its Pantheon-like dome and freestanding columns—for the greater glory of God and the Hapsburg dynasty.

FROM *Austria* BY TONI SCHNEIDERS, PUBLISHED BY THAMES AND HUDSON, LTD.

As the Baroque style spread from parent Italy across Europe, far-flung regions added their own variations to it. In northwestern Spain the twelfth-century cathedral of Santiago de Compostela, famed place of pilgrimage to the tomb of Saint James, was enriched soon after 1700 with a new façade (left) whose tumultuous ornament conveys a Spanish love of intensity and incrustation. Across the continent, on a cliff above the Danube near the edge of Bohemia, Jakob Prandtauer incorporated Eastern onion-tower motifs in his majestic Benedictine monastery of Melk (above).

For a Baroque grandee it was not enough that his palace be spacious; it must also be dramatic and exuberant inside and out. So he built rhapsodic gardens and swirling stairwells that heightened both his budgets and his effects. At vast cost, Philip V of Spain (1683–1746) commissioned the fountains (below) at his summer residence at La Granja, only to remark of them moodily, "They cost me three million and kept me amused for three minutes." Provincial princelings let their imaginations soar too: the Waldburg family in the 1700's embellished their south German seat at Wurzach with a central staircase (right) whose magnificence, rising through tiers of balustrades, cartouches, urns, and cupids, rivaled that of kings.

INGE MORATH–MAGNUM; (RIGHT) LUDWIG WINDSTOSSER–THE ROY BERNARD CO.

With ten fountains like these, King Philip V's summer gardens outdid Versailles

Wurzach Palace's stairwell was a masterwork of the architect Balthasar Neumann

THE GRANDEURS OF DEATH

No man more ardently voiced both the Baroque age's lust for life and its concern with mortality than England's great love poet and churchman, John Donne (1573–1631). Amorist and mystic, first a raffish young man about town, then a lawyer and envoy, finally Dean of St. Paul's, he set out by astonishing his late Elizabethan contemporaries with lyrics of an entirely new kind—strident, caustic, highly personal, and barbed with tortuous images to convey extremes of passion. Then his passion turned to God, and as the favorite minister of James I and Charles I, he preached of man's fate in a language of whose splendor and soaring imagery this passage, from a "Devotion" written in 1623, is a crowning example:

Nunc lento sonitu dicunt, Morieris.	*Now, this Bell tolling softly for another, saies to me, Thou must die.*

Perchance hee for whom this *Bell* tolls, may be so ill, as that he knowes not it tolls for him; And perchance I may thinke my selfe so much better than I am, as that they who are about mee, and see my state, may have caused it to toll for mee, and I know not that. The *Church* is *Catholike, universall,* so are all her *Actions; All* that she does, belongs to *all.* When she *baptizes a child,* that action concernes mee; for that child is thereby connected to that *Head* which is my *Head* too, and engraffed into that *body*, whereof I am a *member.* And when she *buries a Man,* that action concernes me: All *mankinde* is of one *Author*, and is one *volume*; when one Man dies, one *Chapter* is not *torne* out of the *booke*, but *translated* into a better *language*; and every *Chapter* must be so *translated; God* emploies several *translators*; some peeces are translated by *age*, some by *sicknesse*, some by *warre*, some by *justice*; but *Gods* hand is in every *translation*; and his hand shall binde up all our scattered leaves againe, for that *Librarie* where every *booke* shall lie open to one another: As therefore the *Bell* that rings to a *Sermon*, calls not upon the *Preacher* onely, but upon the *Congregation* to come; so this *Bell* calls us all: but how much more mee, who am brought so neere the *doore* by this *sicknesse*.

There was a *contention* as farre as a *suite* (in which both *pietie* and *dignitie, religion,* and *estimation*, were mingled), which of the religious *Orders* should ring to *praiers* first in the *Morning*; and it was *determined*, that *they should ring first that rose earliest.* If we understand aright the *dignitie* of this *Bell* that tolls for our *evening prayer,* wee would bee glad to make it ours, by rising early, in that *application*, that it might bee ours, as wel as his, whose indeed it is. The *Bell* doth toll for him that *thinkes* it doth; and though it *intermit againe,* yet from that *minute*, that that occasion wrought upon him, hee is united to *God.* Who casts not up his *Eye* to the *Sunne* when it rises? but who takes off his *Eye* from a *Comet* when that breakes out? Who bends not his *eare* to any *bell*, which upon any occasion rings? but who can remove it from that *bell*, which is passing a *peece of himselfe* out of this *world*? No man is an *Iland*, intire of itselfe; every man is a peece of the *Continent*, a part of the *maine*; if a *Clod* bee washed away by the *Sea, Europe* is the *lesse*, as well as if a *Promontorie* were, as well as if a *Mannor* of thy *friends* or of *thine owne* were; any mans *death* diminishes *me*, because I am involved in *Mankinde*; And therefore never send to know for whom the *bell* tolls; It tolls for *thee.*

A Paris church was decked out like a stage for this pompe funèbre *celebrating in 1672 Chancellor Pierre Séguier's passage into eternity.*

A DELIGHT

Despite wars and upheavals, the era after 1600 pursued its love of show and theater in a brilliance of masques, operas, pageants, ballets, parades. New-found technical ingenuity was called in to invent movable scenery and stage machinery able to conjure up demons, suspend chariots in mid-air, or represent hell's fires. Every larger court had its fireworks and rearing stage monsters moved by pulleys. Molière and Corneille collaborated on Psyché, *a "spectacular" featuring Venus descending in a flying contraption. Baroque showmanship, in fact, was more Wagnerian even than Richard Wagner—but lighter in spirit.*

Seated in center foreground, Louis XIV presided in 1664 at a three-day festival for which Molière wrote a new comedy and Lully composed ballet music. The climax, in

BULLOZ

Demons disport themselves amid smoldering stage ruins in this Callot engraving of a setting for a play-ballet performed at Florence during the Carnival of 1616.

IN SPECTACLES

BULLOZ

his Versailles gardens, with a palisade of paintings and a stage palace in the background, saw three sea monsters (above) carrying in three leading actresses, thinly clad.

In a pageant of 1662, the Duc de Guise rode accoutred as an "American king." Far left, opposite: young Louis XIV danced thus costumed in a court ballet, 1653.

THE BETTMANN ARCHI

Provincial Munich provided a grandiose setting for the production of Steffani's opera Servio Tullio *on the occasion of Prince-Elector Max Emmanuel's marriage in 1685.*

A SPLENDOR OF MUSIC

Perhaps the ultimate fulfillment of the Baroque spirit lay in music, which it revolutionized and carried to hitherto undreamed-of heights. New instruments, new forms, new masters followed one another in dazzling profusion, and the culminating figure of Johann Sebastian Bach personifies musically the age's leading traits: its exuberance, intensity, limitless exploration, intricacy, piety, and splendor of effect. The manuscript page above of his Prelude in B minor for organ, with its swirling arches of notes, itself suggests a piece of bold Baroque architecture. Music was also linked to ceremony and made the occasion of pomp and circumstance. At right, a painting by Giovanni Paolo Pannini records a concert in 1729 in the palace of the French embassy at Rome on the occasion of the birth of the dauphin, son of Louis XV, at which the work performed was the opera La Contesa dei Numi *by the now-forgotten composer Leonardo Vinci (1690–1730). The extreme elaboration of the design places this scene on the threshold of the next epoch—the Rococo.*

LOUVRE–GIRAUDON

TEXT CONTINUED FROM PAGE 50

la vida es sueño; Y los sueños, sueños son" (that all life is a dream, and the dreams are dreams as well).

The clear, sharply defined surfaces of Renaissance bodies melt into the twilight of ever-changing, illusory shadows: "What is life? Frenzy! What is life? An illusion, a shadow, a fiction!" The spaces of church interiors, once luminous and sharply defined, become ever more complex and agitated—the walls seem to vanish as they become more wavy and curving, and the ceilings rise and soar into the infinite as the great Baroque painters provide ever more distant vistas of heaven and of God Almighty. It is a world of beauteous sheen, of semblances and the effervescent foam of passing forms.

Of all the means of expression which man has developed to give vent to his feelings in beautiful and communicable form, music is the most inward, and at the same time the most intensely emotional. It is also usually the last to achieve stylistic fulfillment in any given age. The greatest musicians of the Baroque—Bach, Handel, and Vivaldi—all belong to the end of the seventeenth and the first half of the eighteenth century. The work of these towering geniuses has until recently made music lovers forget the magnificent achievements with which Baroque music was ushered in by Gabrieli, Monteverdi, and the other exponents of the *stilo nuovo.*

It was these extraordinary Italians of the early seventeenth century who abandoned the formal approach of Renaissance music, as it had been written by Palestrina and Sweelinck, for the more expressive monodic style which animates their operas and oratorios and the vast body of organ music written by such masters as Frescobaldi, Gesualdo, and Carissimi. It is also the Baroque that brings the full flowering of instrumental music, in many ways the most unique cultural achievement of the West. And among all the instruments invented and perfected in this musical age, the organ was the most important. The organ, with its infinite variety of voices and moods, embodies the Baroque spirit at its best and most creative. Only recently has the superiority of these great instruments with their vast tonal potentialities been appreciated again, and the early art of organ-building been restudied and revived.* The D minor Toccata and Fugue of Bach has rightly been proclaimed the pinnacle of organ form, building as it does an infinite range of musical expression out of the simplest elements.

But the organ was only the most mighty of the instruments that the Baroque age perfected. The unique achievement of Bach was his exploration of the furthest potentialities of all instruments, keyboard and string. One loves the great Italians from Frescobaldi to Vivaldi and Scarlatti; yet it was Bach who composed, especially in his solo suites, what was destined to become "the final page," so to speak, for each instrument. In his Brandenburg concertos he also achieved the ultimate in polyphonic wealth of contrast of instruments, although his highest accomplishment remains the combination of these instruments with the human voice, both singly and in choral masses, in his great Passions. Only the *Messiah* of Handel can be compared to them. Yet it is too often forgotten that Bach in these works, too, was a master at perfecting what others had begun. Of one of these early oratorios, written in 1628 by Orazio Benevoli, it has been said that it is "as if Bernini's Spanish staircase and his gigantic colonnades before St. Peter's had been transformed into music."

In contemplating the six generations from 1570 to 1750 who lived and created the Baroque style in the arts, music, and letters, one always goes back to the historical setting. At the beginning of the age, men could and did still believe that the medieval world might be revived. The Counter Reformation, no less than the political ambitions of the house of Hapsburg, suggested the possibility of re-establishing the unity of Christendom. By the end of the seventeenth century, all this world was dead. The Holy Roman Empire had been declared a monstrosity by Grotius, one of the greatest jurists of the day, and the Church had ceased to be a primary factor in European politics.

Long in the making, the modern state now became firmly and irrevocably established in Europe and, above all, in France, where Richelieu, Mazarin, and Louis XIV—three of the greatest actors who strutted across the stage of the *Theatrum Europaeum*—built the *Etat* which was to dominate Western thought until constitutionalism, spreading from England, triumphed in the nineteenth century and foreshadowed the world of today. Three primary events which filled the first half of the seventeenth century mark this emergence: the Thirty Years' War (1618–1648), the victory of France over Spain as the predominant power in Europe, and the English revolution and civil war (1642–1660). Later, the successful turning back of the Turks and the entrance of Russia into the European concert mark the end of the century. The emergence of great powers follows the emergence of the modern state, and between them they provide the political setting for this marvelous age. Throughout runs the obsessive struggle for power—the era's *libido dominandi,* as the pale language of psychoanalysis calls it in our day. John Milton's Satan was perhaps as striking a portrait of Baroque man as any the age created: "aspiring / To set himself in glory above his peers, / He trusted to have equalled the Most High. . . ." Yet he was hurled to the depths, and at last he seems to echo Shakespeare:

"We are such stuff
As dreams are made on, and our little life
Is rounded with a sleep."

A student of the arts as well as of the history of political thought, Carl J. Friedrich is Eaton Professor of the Science of Government at Harvard University and the author of many books, including The Age of the Baroque *(Harpers, 1952).*

*See "The King of Instruments Returns," by E. Power Biggs, in HORIZON for March, 1960.

American Mores at Mid-Century: V

AFTER ABUNDANCE, WHAT?

By ERIC LARRABEE

AFTER ABUNDANCE, WHAT?

Ill at ease in Zion, the beneficiary of American affluence looks up from his cornucopia and yearns for a sense of purpose. The hard-bitten ideals of past eras of scarcity no longer serve him. Yet a surfeit of things material is increasing a demand for things spiritual and intangible

In a short story called "The Midas Touch," the science-fiction writer Frederik Pohl has succeeded in posing—and, to a degree, resolving—one of the critical dilemmas of the mid-twentieth century. Pohl imagines a future in which industrial production has been entirely taken over by robots, while human beings—in order to keep the economic machinery going—are required only to consume. But consume they must. In this hypothetical society, consumption has become obligatory; everyone has a quota—clothes, food, car, recreation, and the rest—and is severely penalized for failing to live up to it.

Privilege, in Pohl's fantasy, consists of the right *not* to consume. The lower classes are forced to engorge the most; they have to eat too much and drive around in overdecorated automobiles. Only those of the highest rank are allowed to be thin, or have unpretentious possessions, or do any work. Pohl's hero is in difficulty since he has fallen behind in using up his allotment, but in a moment of aberration he hits on the solution not only of his problem but of society's. He puts robots to consuming for him; and when this is discovered, far from being punished, he is greeted as a savior. His idea is universally adopted and the Golden Age arrives.

Like much science fiction, Mr. Pohl's story is a work of pungent social criticism. What he describes is recognizably related to the Era of Consumption in which we now live, and his parody of inverse snobbery about ostentation is only slightly overdrawn from reality. This state of affairs has been coming upon us for some time and has been given many names: Stuart Chase called it "The Economy of Abundance" in 1934, and John Kenneth Galbraith called it "The Affluent Society" in 1958. We may always have been a "People of Plenty," as David Potter characterized Americans in 1954, but what these several writers have been saying is that a bend was rounded into a new human landscape—Stuart Chase dated it at about 1920—when consumption became more difficult than production. Ever since, we have been struggling to make sense of a new and unmapped environment.

This phenomenon has been described so often as to need no further clichés on the subject here. Suffice it to say that Abundance has brought such sharp increases in the conventional measures of social activity as to suggest not merely a change in quantity but in quality. It is a different kind of society. If I may be allowed just one example, it is a society with less and less use for that venerable institution, the hock shop. In the past fifteen years, the number of pawnshops in Boston has declined from 82 to 44, and in a fraction of that time the number in New York has dropped from 135 to 120. "We're getting killed by lots of things," says one proprietor. "The easy credit, the easy bank loans, installment buying, credit associations, withholding tax, the ten-cent checking account—they all ruined the pawn business."

It should be understood, of course, even if Pohl's science-fiction story did not underline the point, that the Abundant Society is not identical with the millennium. It has not necessarily made people happier; it has merely changed the conditions under which happiness is pursued. Many of its features are problematical or obscure, while others are indistinguishable from those of hectic boom times, and no less distasteful. Carl Sandburg has contemptuously referred to our own day as one of "fat-dripping prosperity," and many others share the dissatisfaction with it that Russell Lynes summed up in his book *A Surfeit of Honey* (1957): "Prosperity produces not only plenty but curiously empty values and a national uneasiness. . . . Cars get gaudier; hi-fi sets get hi-er; beer-can openers become mink-bearing, open fields are swallowed up to make future slums, slums are torn down to make parking lots; pastures become drive-in movies; drive-in movie operators provide heaters so that one does not have to desert his status symbol even in winter."

The "national uneasiness" has, if anything, increased since Lynes wrote, and currently it is on the edge of becoming a political issue. Abundance is whimsical; it descends unevenly, slighting a necessity here to bestow a luxury there. It has failed to abolish poverty, let alone sin; and it satisfies private demands—as Galbraith and now Walter Lippmann have insisted—sooner than public ones. It will provide tail fins and television sooner than parks, schools, or unpolluted air and water. In a recent Herblock cartoon, titled "Split-level living," the private consumer lolls in witless extravagance while, on a floor below, figures labeled Education, Defense, and Health and Welfare starve in squalor. Here are the makings of a good argument over the question of how national wealth is to be deployed, and the New York *Times* has begun to call it a "great debate."

Its central antagonist so far has been Dr. Raymond J. Saulnier, chairman of the President's Council of Economic Advisers, who, in his testimony before a Congressional committee last year, let drop some words which have currently been much quoted. "As I understand an economy," he said, "its ultimate purpose is to produce more consumer goods. This is the goal. This is the object of everything we are working at: to produce things for consumers." This concise and vigorous statement was naturally seized upon by Democratic economists as proof that the Administration was deliberately skimping on national needs in order to promote the very riot of private indulgence that has been so much in evidence. Dr. Saulnier has since gone to some pains to indicate that he was being miscast ("I have been represented as being the high priest of gadgets") and that by "things for consumers" he meant also schools, roads, and hospitals, but by the time he said so the issues were too well joined for it to matter.

Part of the debate is the thoroughly old-fashioned one over government spending: Should there be more or less? Part of it is over questions of fact or professional judgment: Do we have "enough" defense, whatever that is, or have our cities decayed "enough" to need massive rebuilding? Part of it, too (as James Reston suggests), may be a difference of temperament, whether one puts consolidation or innovation first, or a difference in the moral point of view which emphasizes material things as against those of the spirit. But part of it also is a more profound difference over the nature of Abundance, where it came from and where it is going, and here the battle lines are by no means so sharply drawn. This is the debate that Stuart Chase saw coming a quarter of a century ago. "Presently the western world," he wrote, "will split between the Scarcity men and the Abundance men. . . ."

Scarcity has obviously been the state of most of mankind for most of its existence, and the attitudes that accompany Scarcity are deeply ingrained. Generations of attachment to the land, of being rooted in the soil and dependent on it for survival, bred a close and canny husbanding of resources. It set the mold in which many of our ideas of individual initiative, effectiveness, and reliability were formed. But with the coming of modern urban industrialism, the habits of Scarcity have had to be unlearned. Once consumption becomes a good in itself—not to speak of the economy's "goal"—then the ethic of hard work and hard money no longer applies.

Under Abundance, for example, too much thrift can become a social vice. To hold back money and keep it out of circulation may be worse for the society than to spend it and keep the wheels of production turning. Industrialism is a multiplier; it can create so much more, more of whatever is needed, that the word "waste" tends to become meaningless. What matters is the process, and the process may involve "wastefulness" of a kind that Americans have always been willing to tolerate. What does it matter if the forests are stripped from Wisconsin, provided there are houses on the Great Plains? What does it matter if a few scoundrels grow too rich, provided the railroads get through to the Pacific?

Waste is relative. Once industrialism takes further hold, what appeared to be "waste" may disappear. Scarcely a decade ago, in Texas, more natural gas was "flared away" (that is, burned) than was piped out of the state; it wasn't worth the trouble of keeping. In the copper mines of Northern Rhodesia are areas that used to be marked "barren"—no good: too much uranium. Given the incentive, by-products become raw materials—the refuse of one Wisconsin paper plant can produce half the world's supply of artificial vanilla; and it is an apt industrial legend that once upon a time a group of chemists, on a bet, actually did make a silk purse out of a sow's ear.

"... a Scarcity man ... Herbert Hoover"

"... an Abundance man ... Franklin Roosevelt"

Belief in consumption, in addition, requires belief in waste. If it is desirable, in itself, for more people continually to consume more things, then it is also desirable for those things to be worn out and thrown away as rapidly as possible. If it is good for everyone to own an electric can opener, then it is still better for everyone to own a new one next year. And if all of this conflicts head-on with the traditional faith, with its call to careful workmanship and solid worth, then one or the other should have to give—or so you would think.

Stuart Chase saw that it was possible for people to profess the principles of Scarcity while observing those of Abundance, but he thought it would become less and less possible, and in this he was wrong. Chase's idea of a Scarcity man was Herbert Hoover; of an Abundance man, Franklin Roosevelt; and he would certainly have been surprised to know that two decades later a national administration would be asserting the doctrines of the former while, without embarrassment, imitating the latter's practice. The irony of Dr. Saulnier's position is that he was caught up publicly in an inconsistency which everyone else commits in private. Theoretically, you cannot believe in consumption—as Dr. Saulnier believes—and be opposed to tail fins, for the belief implies, and justifies, the consequence. In principle, you cannot live in both worlds at once—though that is what most of us actually do.

We live, that is, not in one economy, but two: an economy of Abundance yet one also of Scarcity. The latter may seem an unfair label for what is also known by less harsh-sounding names—the complex of meanings, for example, which William H. Whyte, Jr., in *The Organization Man,* includes under the phrase "Protestant Ethic." Yet "Protestant" is an equally unfair shorthand term—by way of Max Weber and R. H. Tawney—for values and business techniques in which Catholics have shared as largely as Calvinists. So I will use "Scarcity," for all its connotations, to identify an ethical system under which success is understood to result from effort, and effort expects to be rewarded; and the equally unfair word "Abundance" to denote that other universe whose "ultimate purpose," in Dr. Saulnier's words, is to keep the tidal wave of consumer goods in motion.

The two economies have come to co-exist, encompassing and interpenetrating each other, but always distinct—like the two tribes in northern Nigeria, the Fulani and the Hausa, which live scattered throughout the same geographic area while retaining their separate identities. There is a world of Scarcity and one of Abundance. The standards of one do not apply to the other: money in one has different value than in the other; success and reputation in one may, in the other, be non-negotiable. Yet the same individual may be called upon to cross the boundary between the two economies dozens of times a day, possibly in mid-sentence, and may in fact be asked to perform in both at once. A man may very often have an office life of Abundance and a home life of Scarcity, or be paid in Scarcity money and be obliged to consume on an Abundance scale.

A friend of mine, to take one instance, works for an Abundance organization whose parent company inclines toward

Scarcity. His part of the outfit operates in New York, in high Madison Avenue style, dealing largely with imponderables like talent and public opinion. It happens, by historical accident, that the higher echelon which owns and directs this gaudy subsidiary grew up outside of New York, immersed in manufacturing, handling the nuts-and-bolts side of the trade where much of the money still is. According to my informant, one of the most agreeable prerogatives of his job is to watch what happens when a new vice-president comes down from the boondocks to check up on operations in the sinful city—and discovers to his astonishment the delights of a corner office, long lunch hours, and pretty secretaries. Change of allegiance, under these circumstances, is rapidly accomplished.

Abundance value comes from keeping consumption going. Advertising is its characteristic industry, and the entertainment business—which serves a similar purpose by surrounding high consumption with an atmosphere of cheerfulness—sets many of its styles. The greatest Abundance value is conferred on the evanescent, on that which is most quickly consumed—especially personality, or mere celebrity. Income for writers, as an illustration, tends to be in inverse ratio to the permanence of their product. Writers for television comedians, whose work is fragile and quickly forgotten, live in the Abundance economy. Poets, whose work is likely to be more durable, are paid in Scarcity money, if at all.

All money spent in Miami Beach is Abundance money. ("Down here, sir," as the bellhop said to the man who wanted change for a dollar, "a dollar *is* change.") Money earned by people who work with their hands is Scarcity money. What was once a simple disparity between rich and poor (the money of the rich was different; there was so much more of it) is now a disparity between two standards of worth, operating side by side, so to speak, in the same market. Realistically speaking, most of us pay and are paid in a mixture of both currencies: our lives are miniature versions of the national dilemma, and we are never quite sure when we are supposed to be putting out or when we can take it easy. The trick, of course, is not to be caught spending income from one's best Scarcity efforts for anything priced according to the Abundance motto—which is: "It's only money."

An extreme example of Abundance value is, of course, tax money—money which will be lost unless it is spent, either for charity or expenses or on some complicated legalistic maneuver by which an apparent loss can be converted into an actual gain. These are, in effect, government subsidies for certain forms of behavior, a certain lavishness of performance, which has thereby become accepted practice. Further down the line are the more overt forms of subsidy, ranging through the Welfare State devices for supporting entire social classes beyond their means to the cost-plus contracts of the Defense Department which have raised missile, electronic, and aircraft manufacturers to the status of state-supported public utilities. Over the vast sector of these activities, the so-called "discipline of the market-place" is largely inoperative.

In personal terms, the change has been one from competitiveness to what David Riesman, in *The Lonely Crowd,* calls "antagonistic co-operation"—from Whyte's Protestant Ethic to what he calls the "social ethic." Gone are the days of the clerk who arrives early and stays late, like the young Andrew Carnegie, conspicuously outdoing his peers in zeal and in his indifference to their antagonism. Rarer now are the lights burning night-long in the downtown law factories and fewer the week-long "charettes" in the offices of architects. The mode is to displace one's equals without demoralizing them, to slide gracefully by into a higher slot on the seniority escalator without rate-busting, or attracting undue attention, or losing that mellow but guarded affection which teammates are supposed to profess for one another. The premium is on Nice Guys, and especially on the one who can out-nice all the rest.

For we are still, Abundance notwithstanding, a competitive society. Sewell Avery was perhaps the last *real* Scarcity businessman—the photograph of him being carted out of his office by two soldiers may someday serve as a symbol for the end of his era—and it is particularly ironical that *Fortune* magazine, which has done so much to shame the rough-and-tough executive out of existence, should now ruefully lament his passing. But the picture of all-encompassing benevolence can easily be exaggerated. There are still businesses red in tooth and claw, where the word about Togetherness has not yet penetrated and where the soothing sirup of the human-relations experts is not dispensed in the operating echelons.

There are still enclaves of Scarcity, like Detroit, where the harsh law of the economic jungle is still considered to be in effect and a division manager, for example, will be allowed, at most, two unsuccessful years before being put out to pasture with the other discarded models. It is one of the paradoxes of the automotive industry, itself so effective an agent in the transformation of American life along Abundance lines, that it clings nostalgically to the Scarcity ideal of conduct, priding itself on nineteenth-century hardness and frowning severely at any evidence of advanced ideas, such as sympathy for labor or foreign-built cars, on the part of its aspiring junior managers.

There is also, throughout the country, a vast network composed of hapless people who—whether because they desire to or simply know no better—go on striving to be effective and reliable out of all proportion to the reward such activity can possibly earn them. This is the Protestant Ethic Underground, invisible to the outsider but known as a matter of necessity to anyone else whose job requires him to get anything done. Here and there in the skilled handicrafts are the compulsive craftsmen—most of them (regrettably) immigrants and most (even more regrettably) getting on in years—who regard shoddy workmanship as so sinful that they have to be coerced into "modernizing" and debasing their ancient methods. By some mysterious process, also, we are

". . . two unsuccessful years before being put out to pasture with the other discarded models"

still producing new generations of men and women whose self-respect requires them to fly in the face of economic self-interest and be efficient, trustworthy, and conscientious.

They do so, that is, to the extent that they fail in devotion to Dr. Saulnier's idol. The only reason the Abundant Society works is that a sufficient portion of its membership does not believe in it.

The only reason it exists at all is that our ancestors did not believe in it. Abundance was born in Scarcity, born because of Scarcity. The Protestant Ethic was the product of a harsh and uncompromising experience in which failure was no idle threat. To succor the unfortunate poor was permissible as charity, but if carried too far it would undermine their incentive and resolve. Just a little depression, just a touch of starvation now and then, was thought to be a useful reminder of the inalterable order of nature which had decreed that only the fittest should survive. In this hard school were formed those habits of precision and industriousness on which technological culture depends. Out of the horror of this detour into moral vacuum came those drives toward social betterment which scattered the largesse of mass production more evenly, and of which our own petty gestures toward reform are the last faint ripples from a once-mighty wave.

But how are we to retain such drives, now that the overt need for them has vanished? How far can we coast on impulses set in motion many generations ago? One of the most immediate by-products of Abundance, as Robert L. Heilbroner writes in *The Future as History,* "is the gradual elimination of a group hitherto so prevalent as to be beyond need of notice, and so indispensable as to be simply taken for granted—the great mass of anonymous men on whose generalized willingness to work the high edifices of civilization have been built. It is this group which abundance slowly causes to disappear. The diffusion of well-being down into the lower ranks of society gradually obliterates the line between those who have not and who must, and those who have and who therefore need not. Society is increasingly composed of those who need not."

So on, up through the ranks, until ultimately the time comes when there will be some jobs that no one can be got to fill. And so also, conceivably, there can come to exist the society which needs not, and cannot be got to bestir itself from its fully equipped contentment.

Perhaps—and, for such gently reared good liberals as myself, this would be a most painful concession—the exponents of Scarcity were right all along. Perhaps a minimum of brute indifference to suffering is essential to maintain social vitality. Perhaps Abundance is a self-destructive ideal. Having attained it, perhaps we are doomed to join Toynbee's collection of dying civilizations, to be no more than a new set of actors in the age-old drama of surfeit and decay, of the mailed boot coming up the staircase of history—in Talleyrand's phrase—and the velvet slipper going down. If so, we can at least draw some consolation from the fact that the Soviets are apparently prey to the same unhappy thought when they contemplate the stern, dedicated self-sacrifice of the Chinese Communist students who come to Moscow. "The irony of history," a young Russian told George Sherman of the London *Sunday Observer,* "is that the more prosperous we become, the more bourgeois we are. We love our comforts, our refinements, and we want more. But the farther West we move, the farther we move from the Socialist East."

Here in our own country, at any rate, we seem to have constructed a machine which can satisfy wants faster than it can create them, yet is dependent on wants in order to keep going. We are running low on our supply of utopian dreams, while at the same time we have become too worldly-wise to be attracted by farfetched—and hence exhilarating—objectives. We are so doubtful about national aims that the President has appointed a commission to find out what they are. As David Riesman puts it, "serious discussion of the future is just what is missing in the United States. . . . There is liberation in plenty itself, up to a point. And yet I think we fear the future's opacity, and try not to pierce it with concrete plans. . . . What we fear to face is more than total destruction: it is total meaninglessness. . . ."

We have arrived, in other words, at a point where aims that fall short of the utopian will no longer do. Even the "great debate" that Professor Galbraith and Dr. Saulnier have set in motion may simply be swallowed up in still more Abundance. If the economy increases during the 1960's at an annual rate of 4 per cent, which seems to be the figure most often mentioned, then there will be four billion dollars more a year for public spending without any change whatever in the balance between public and private. If, moreover, there were to be reductions in Federal support of either agriculture or armament, then the fantastic flood of revenue would be enough to do all that the most spendthrift advocates of Abundance have demanded, and more besides. Highway programs and the like would not even begin to dent this surplus of national energy, even if—following the inspired suggestion of former Governor Earl Long of Louisiana—we were to have *two* complete highways systems, the second reserved for drunks.

Since the advent of Abundance, it has become difficult to be too utopian. The physicist John Rader Platt has pointed out that the late nineteenth- and early twentieth-century writers of imaginative fiction like Jules Verne and H. G. Wells, straining themselves to foresee the unimaginable, were rarely able to project their readers more than fifteen or twenty years into the future. Since twenty years may elapse between a young scientist's education and his maturity, this now means that every scientific generation must cope with problems for which it is considerably unprepared; and hence Platt argues that science itself is in genuine need of poets—or, at a minimum, men and women schooled like poets to stretch their imaginations to the utmost.

What Abundance requires are wants that cannot be too easily satisfied—that are, best of all, insatiable—and there is only one category of wants that fits this definition. Only the intangible wants are infinite. Only the pursuit of aesthetic, moral, or intellectual ends can go on indefinitely; and they are, therefore, the only goals that an Abundant society can seek without devitalizing itself. To put it another way, the oversupply of things material increases, rather than diminishes, the demand for things spiritual. As Mary McCarthy once wrote, "Until you have had a washing machine, you cannot imagine how little difference it will make to you." A society overendowed with gadgets cannot long escape the knowledge that gadgets are not enough.

We need not only outrageous and "impossible" objectives—a dream of alabaster cities, perhaps, set in a fertile countryside which they do not demean—but we need to take them seriously. Hitherto, in the conflict between the dual economies of Abundance and Scarcity, we have grown accustomed to allocating Abundance only to certain limited sectors. But the division between public and private is not nearly so significant as that between realistic and impractical; we allocate Abundance mainly to the latter; we think of it as primarily appropriate for those things which we do not truly need or intend to use, such as Las Vegas or the Strategic Air Command, while Scarcity prevails over anything "real." Something the nation really requires, like an army that could fight a limited war, gets the short end of the stick. When it comes to our man-made surroundings—for example, the hard goods that make up the environment in which our lives go forward—we are still cost-accounting them as though Scarcity ruled supreme, and they look it. Whenever new plans are made, in this age when even the highest architectural style is spartan and severe, there then comes a time when budgets demand that they be trimmed and pared back; and you may be certain that the first qualities to be sacrificed are the intangibles like beauty, amenity, and humanity. What we aspire to is mean enough; what we build are its bare bones.

The dialogue between Scarcity and Abundance is also the medium in which we carve out personalities and careers, and it puts as great a challenge to individuals as to society. The demands of Scarcity were at least categorical: to build an empire, settle a continent, make a fortune, write a masterpiece, or be a "great man"—these may have been unattainable for the majority, but they were clear. If you chose to respond to them, no one was in any doubt as to what you were doing. But the demands of Abundance are for skill, perspective, considerateness, and—hardest of all—for individuality strong enough not to need the old-fashioned, monomaniac supports. While Scarcity prevailed, individuality was a forced growth, a neurotic insistence on the self to the exclusion of all others, and often enough it would bloom into monstrous ego. That kind of "greatness," for all its sharply edged power, is a closed chapter in social evolution; and now we are obliged to get on, and to have courage and decency, without it.

It is easy enough to rage at conformity, at Other-directedness, or at the Organization Man, just as it is easy to attribute to a bygone era the virtues of fierce inner integrity that we reproach ourselves for not possessing. But in doing so we risk ignoring how much better a life it is that organization has made possible, how much wiser our sense of the world's interdependence has made us, and how much more decently people now must treat each other in their daily routines. It is easier to ridicule bureaucracy, or Togetherness, or the Suburbs than it is to remember that in sum total they represent, for the great majority, an enlargement in the range of human possibility. Perhaps the price is too high, but before we are quite so quick to reach that conclusion we should remind ourselves what Scarcity was really like—how crabbed, and mean, and bitter, and hopeless it could be. Autonomy for the individual, at any event, cannot be recaptured in terms of Scarcity's archaic and irrelevant code, but must be constructed anew, to suit the conditions of a more subtle, complicated, and dissatisfied time.

The intention of these five articles, of which this is the last, has been to describe some of the surface aspects of contemporary society, but in such a way as to show the more durable outlines of the human condition not far beneath. We are not all that unique—and the combined outcome of our social fluidity, our cultural free-for-all, and our uneasy opulence is to throw the individual back on his or her inner resources, which are, on the average, not much greater or lesser than they have been before. In this state the long record of the past—the growth of knowledge and the accumulation of art, music, and literature—is almost as relevant as anything the present might say. In some ways I have the feeling of having written an overlong advertisement for a liberal-arts education.

This is not intended to be simply another bouquet for the humanities, the introspection of the artist and his audience, or the traditional injunction to "know thyself." The opportunity of this era is not only for the self, but for innumerable selves—all of them we can accommodate—and it is in this that we have left precedent behind. Until our dirty and disreputable industrial civilization came along, even the modest range of cultural experience that the arts represent was foreclosed to all but a tiny minority. Individualism as we know it, as a possibility for the many, did not exist until modern times. A society that makes individualism possible is a new thing under the sun, and one that could endure would be our most admirable artifact.

We need—well, all right, what do we need? We need—as who does not?—to be as little children and be born again. We need to dare greatly, more greatly than we have ever dared. We need a good fifty-cent cigar. We need to be less impressed with our own helplessness. The theme of this series has been self-consciousness—the awareness this generation of Americans has acquired of itself; and one of the inevitable by-products of self-awareness is a sense of futility and of one's own feebleness. We know all too much to enjoy that easygoing optimism which was for so long the trademark of our fellow countrymen. But the challenge is all the greater when the odds are known. Henry Miller, in the *Wisdom of the Heart,* says that real progress always has elements in it of the blind and instinctive, like a leap in the dark. What is asked of us is yet more difficult—like a leap in the light.

Abundance, to say it once again, is not a social soporific but a call on society and its members to transcend themselves. It leaves us no alternative but to think; and I have nowhere found this better stated than in a remark of Gregory Corso, the beatnik poet, to Art Buchwald. Mr. Corso was explaining that poetry was taking over the country, that soon the bankers would be beatniks too and open the vaults, and then we would all be rich. "It won't be long," he said, "before everyone will sit in bed and eat big fat pies. They got machines now to do the work. People got to start thinking. That's what's going to save us. Everyone staying in bed eating big fat pies and thinking."

There won't be anything else to do.

Illustrations by Marc Simont

The Making of a Master

Just forty as he completes his twenty-fifth year of performance, Isaac Stern has been called "the youngest of the great musicians"

By THEODORE H. WHITE

The lights fade in the hall. A thickset man, head bowed, face grave, weaves quickly forward through the thicket of instruments and, suddenly, is present. He pauses, then tucks his violin beneath his chin. His head cocks to one side. Above the restless rustling of the crowded hall he is listening to something he alone can hear. As he listens, a hush falls. Then, with a half-nod to the conductor, who towers above the orchestra, he indicates he has heard and is ready. The conductor's baton falls. Bow touches string. And the magic of sound drenches the listeners.

It is not often the magic is heard with such clarity—serene yet commanding, passionate yet utterly clear. Nor can the audience know exactly how such magic is made. The audience cannot have seen this same man that morning, dressed in black turtle-neck sweater, gathering about him this same orchestra in the empty rehearsal hall, nor has it observed this now-serene face tense and perplexed. It has not seen this man pause in mid-phrase, then frown, then halt, then whisper with the conductor as the orchestra waits; nor has it seen him begin again, with orchestra and conductor following, then wince and pause again, then resume—the face of the fiddler suddenly clear in an enormous glow as a new silhouette of melody arises out of the dissonant sound as orchestra and artist sail ahead in joy to the next passage, the next frown, the next halt. It has not seen him, still dissatisfied, call the departing musicians back in a circle around him to explain what he plays with them as a threnody for the death of a girl of eighteen whom the composer has tried to memorialize forever. It has not listened to him softly persuading, softly explaining, finally winning the suspicious, reluctant men of the orchestra to understanding and willingness to try again.

None of this can the audience have seen. All that is here now is a finished magic. The audience perceives chiefly an adventure before it on the stage—with precise and powerful fingers the violinist is exploring on his instrument the unreal sounds in the composer's imagination, marrying his own personality to that of the composer to give birth to a public beauty. It is not the music and the sound alone that make the adventure—it is the personality above the harmony. This is what makes the audience lean forward as the body of the fiddler sways toward it, extending a pool of magnetism out from the stage, over the pit, up to the farthest balcony.

For twenty-five years now, this particular sound has been swelling in the ears of listeners from America to Australia, from Asia to Europe, to reach what is now recognized as a master sound which only half a dozen men of this century have drawn from the fiddle. It is the music of Isaac Stern. And if there is triumph in it, it is not that of one man alone. Borne with it is another triumph—that of an entire culture and a new community in the world of music. For the story of Isaac Stern is, perhaps, just as much the story of the development and maturing of American music to its present brilliance as it is the story of an individual and his art.

The story starts in a parlor on Green Street, overlooking the Bay from San Francisco's Pacific Heights, as a slender adolescent saws away at a violin before a transplanted Russian concert violinist. The adolescent is Stern, and his teacher is Naoum Blinder.

It is well to pause for a moment at Blinder—a warm, dedicated, gifted teacher. By such people as Blinder, the arts, the sciences, and the music of the Old World were all seeded in America to take new form. Blinder had grown up in Eastern Europe in a musical culture dominated by the virtuosi of the "Russian violin." The Russian violin, and that specific style of playing which originated beyond the Carpathians, has dominated the concert halls of the world for almost half a century. The great virtuosi of this school glory some in an icy precision, others in an overflowing lush emotion—yet all are bound together by a reverence for pure performance that seems to make music a formal challenge to the dexterity of their finger-mechanics and the acuity of their hearing. At its best, this playing becomes a dazzling display of wizardry.

From Blinder, presumably, Stern learned those exact fundamentals of the old school that still form the robust foundation of his playing. But America and San Francisco were already changing Blinder. There was something more fluid and free in Blinder's teaching than a youngster in Russia might have known. In San Francisco's mellow air Blinder had come to stress less the endlessly monotonous scale practice and precision mechanics of the old school than the style which best spoke the emerging personality of the student. From this change of attitude, Stern benefited.

Stern benefited, perhaps, just as much from the good fortune that had caused his parents to bring him to San Francisco before his first birthday. For in the late twenties and early thirties, only San Francisco, outside of New York and Boston, boasted an American audience musically mature enough to invite a Kreisler, a Schnabel, a Rachmaninoff, a Serkin, a Piatigorsky to perform and be fully understood. San Francisco's Opera House brought Melchior, Flagstad, Rethberg, Pons, and Lotte Lehmann to sing. In and about San Francisco's concert stage, opera, and symphony orchestra hummed a world of young music lovers who gave their

PHOTOGRAPHS GJON MILI

emotions to such gods of music as elsewhere in America young people with the same enthusiasm gave theirs to the heroes of sport, jazz, and movies.

Stern cannot say now when it was that music became for him a way of life. He was part of the music crowd, the quartet-playing amateurs, the adoring backstage clusters. He remembers listening to his radio in his room one day as Lily Pons sang her debut in *Lucia* and recalls the tears streaming down his face at her voice, "so high, so thin, so beautiful." But he cannot remember when "the violin came alive under my fingers. No one can remember that," he says. By fifteen he had played his first concert in San Francisco, by seventeen had come his first appearance in New York.

Stern's first appearance in New York, at Town Hall, he recalls as a disaster. He now regards it philosophically, paraphrasing with wry humor one review which ran, "From California, the land of orange juice and sunshine, comes a new prodigy with a big fat G-string and not much else."

Looking back now from the eminence of forty at the performance of his seventeen-year-old self, Stern says that he knew nothing then about the profession of concert violinist; and then he proceeds to explain what that profession is.

The profession of concert violinist is an enormously intricate one; yet the core of the matter is that the artist must sense within himself and transmit an "authority." In some concert artists, this shows as arrogance, in others as a joyous gusto. But essentially it is the quality that makes any star of stage or screen a star. It is a mystic release that permits the person on stage to strip emotions bare and to grapple, naked, with truth and beauty. It requires complete mastery of technique, complete understanding of what the composer or playwright has tried to express—and a knowledge of audiences. For without audience there is no art. Audience is the seat of judgment to which the artist must communicate not fact but emotion; audience is dark faces beyond the footlights whom the artist must conscript into his mood so that finally he and they are one.

This profession Stern learned in the next five and a half years the hard way—the way of coach seats on night trains and highway buses; by auditions before strange conductors of strange orchestras; by growing to understand American audiences at a moment when those audiences, under the tutelage of such titans as Koussevitzky and Toscanini, were growing to understand great music. Today, of course, more admissions are paid to symphony concerts in the United States than to baseball games, but during Stern's apprenticeship such a state of affairs could not be imagined. Learning to know audiences as America learned to know music, Stern began to develop that translucid clarity of expression, that extraordinary ability to communicate, which, along with a native warmth and tone, was soon to stamp his playing.

There is, say many critics, a moment of breakthrough in the life of every performer which may come early (as with a Mozart in his childhood) or late (as with a Rubinstein, breaking out into mastery in his fifties). But whenever it comes, it is the moment when technical proficiency has been completely absorbed in the personality of the performer; when the essence of the man commands the audience just as much, or more, than the music. It is the moment when knowledge and training become so supple and pliable that the artist is completely at home and finally free to be himself. Then, only, can he be judged.

Stern sets this period of "control" which presages breakthrough as occurring in 1942 and early 1943, and the scene as being an old apartment hotel on Manhattan's West Side, called the Oliver Cromwell. Some curious alchemy of affinity had made Stern a friend of many physicists at a time when physicists seemed almost as odd an adornment of American culture as violinists. With one of these physicists, Dr. H. H. Goldsmith (who was soon to depart for work on the monster bomb), Stern had come to share a huge and barren studio, three flights above the elevator shaft, beside the water tower on the roof of the hotel.

There, through most of 1942 and 1943, Stern and Goldsmith developed a free-wheeling circle of friends, half scientists, half musicians. In those early days of the war such scientific luminaries as Szilard, Schwinger, Feld, Freedman—later famous as architects of nuclear devastation and radar technology—were all visitors to this studio. Physicists would wander in late at night, and Goldsmith would wake Stern from sleep to play music. Frantic orgies of sonatas, trios, and quartets would stretch around the clock as professional musicians arrived in the afternoon to play until seven, then left for engagements, to be replaced by others who were

CONTINUED ON PAGE 126

JOE CLARK—RAPHO-GUILLUMETTE

This conversation with one of today's most versatile architects continues the HORIZON series "THE ARTIST SPEAKS FOR HIMSELF"

EERO SAARINEN:

"...something between earth and sky..."

An interview by ALLAN TEMKO

Just off the highway in Birmingham, Michigan—a suburb of Detroit that Sinclair Lewis would have found irresistible—stands a false-front colonial structure that could pass for a drive-in, but happens, in fact, to be the office of Eero Saarinen. From this unlikely looking headquarters have poured forth the remarkable variety of designs for airports, research centers, industrial plants, embassies, public monuments, universities, and churches that have shown Saarinen to be not only the exceptionally talented son of his late father, Eliel—a fine early modernist—but in his own right one of the most powerful and resourceful architects in the world. After Frank Lloyd Wright, Saarinen is the most versatile figure American architecture has produced; and now that Wright is dead, he may well prove to be the chief prophet of the contemporary movement in America.

At a time when a phrase such as "group practice" has entered the language of architecture and buildings appear to be more the work of organizations than of individuals, Saarinen—like his father and Wright before him—stands resolutely for the grand tradition of personal genius in the art of construction. Though his staff has increased from ten to ninety during the past decade and he leans heavily on his partners and associates, there is still "only one designer in the firm of Eero Saarinen & Associates," as one of his assistants remarked; "it's like increasing the size of a bottle—the neck remains, and that's Eero."

Eero Saarinen stands behind a cardboard working model of the new residential colleges he has designed for Yale University.

The office, then, is essentially the atelier of a master; and although it is fortunately free of the narcissistic stage settings of Wright's Taliesin or Le Corbusier's dimly lit den of contemplation, the whole workshop is unmistakably suffused by Saarinen's energetic spirit. There are no frills and, except for a couple of Saarinen's famous pedestal chairs beside the reception desk, few comforts. All the rest is stripped-down working space: the building is a loft, really, separated into offices and drafting rooms by partitions which are painted a neutral white. Saarinen's private office is as plain as a monk's cell, but considerably less neat: the broad desk is likely to be littered with samples of structural materials and dozens of drawings, for like virtually every other major architect, he is a superb and rapid draftsman.

But what distinguishes the Saarinen office from all others is the size and beauty of the cardboard working models which can be seen everywhere (photograph opposite), taking whole rooms to themselves, pushing out into corridors, standing crammed among the drafting tables. These miniature buildings represent, like the capital of Lilliput, a city of the imagination; and to see the range and power of that imagination during a walk through the office—to see, for example, immediately after the romantic towers and irregular courts of the two new Yale colleges he designed this year, the magnificent double row of shaped concrete columns of the Dulles International Airport at Washington and the vast cable-suspended roof slung between them (page 83); or the mirror-glass façades of the Bell Laboratories; or the transparent steel office building of the John Deere Company spanning a wooded valley—is to have a precious insight into the nature of the contemporary world.

At their center, in a rumpled suit, or more likely with his coat off and shirt sleeves rolled, smoking a pipe or cigar, exclaiming "Boy!" when a solution is reached, swearing when checked, Saarinen gives the same impression as the dynamic little buildings: of boundless energy contained by discipline. What he is after, and usually gets, is a "clear statement—an expression."

More than anything else, he claims, this is what modern architecture has lacked. "If you take a church, and siphon out every bit of expression," he asks, "what good is it as a church? Maybe an office building doesn't need any expression, although I'm not at all sure about that."

This credo of the personal and human was spoken slowly, with a soft Finnish accent. (The accent tends to deepen, and the pipe smoke to thicken, when he contends with a vexing design or a difficult client, even though Saarinen came to this country in 1923 at the age of thirteen, after his father had won second prize in the Chicago *Tribune* Tower competition and decided to settle permanently.) But more than the accent, Saarinen retains the graciousness of the creative milieu he knew first in his father's home in Finland, where Gorky, Sibelius, and a host of other artists and intellectuals stayed: it was the best place to visit in that part of the world. In something of the same way, his father made the Cranbrook Academy of Art in Bloomfield Hills, Michigan, an oasis of high culture and artistic responsibility in his adopted part of the Middle West. To understand Eero's work, it is first necessary to drive over the curving country roads, beneath trees, to Eliel's seemingly traditional but intensely personal buildings at Cranbrook; to see the metalsmiths, weavers, furniture makers, and other craftsmen at work in the pleasant studios; to turn a corner and see a space open suddenly between friendly brick walls and water playing in a fountain. Then one must drive on a few minutes longer to the home of Eero and his wife, Aline, the art critic. The century-old, red-brick Victorian farmhouse with its spirited gables and high windows, rising from green lawn and shaded by tall elms, is the kind of "anonymous" architecture Saarinen loves.

For him, the human values are what count fundamentally in buildings. If the new structures of the second half of the twentieth century are potentially as revolutionary, in a profound social sense, as the unprecedented technology of the space age, the venerable art of architecture nevertheless has roots which penetrate to the very foundations of human existence. Could architecture remain a fine art, I asked Eero Saarinen, rather than be transformed into mere engineering? Indeed, can we still think of architecture as an art at all?

SAARINEN: I suppose I've always thought naturally of architecture as one of the fine arts. My father, of course, thought of it as an art. But later I came to think of it as many other things, too. It straddles the arts and the sciences, and this causes some strain, some tension, which makes it different from the other arts. Then, partly because of the scientific side, architecture requires teamwork. There are ninety people in this office and we work as a team. But even in a team you work as an individual.

INTERVIEWER: And that's where the art is all-important?

SAARINEN: Art is the driving force. There is a big to-do about the technology of our age, but there are many ways of using technology. The new Yale colleges could have been walled with straightforward metal panels, but aesthetically it was desirable to find materials which would be sympathetic with the older buildings near them. Stone would have been good, but it seems a little bit cumbersome in our time. So we developed a reinforced concrete wall, placing large stones in the forms and injecting concrete grout under pressure around them. It's a technological wall, not a handicraft wall, but it fits the environment.

INTERVIEWER: Do you consider the environment first when you prepare a design?

EWING GALLOWAY

The much criticized Jefferson Memorial in Washington: a Pantheon-like dome of marble.

SAARINEN: Environment is only part of it. There are three main factors to be considered: a site which demands one thing; a program for the building, which has its own demands; and a spirit of the project, which might demand still something else.

INTERVIEWER: You don't consider the program and the spirit inseparable—that is, you don't think the function, the program of the building itself, determines the form?

SAARINEN: The way people talked about functionalism in the thirties? Does anyone think that way any more? Louis Sullivan didn't mean that at all when he said "form follows function." Function influences but doesn't dictate form.

INTERVIEWER: How did the three factors —site, program, and spirit—work out in the new Yale colleges?

SAARINEN: Well, there the site problem was very pressing. You have strong relations with other permanent buildings, and you have to harmonize with them and create a total environment. The programing, on the other hand, was a comparatively simple problem: you have to house a certain number of students and that had been done pretty well in the past. But the spirit was a very strong and very special problem. One had to think of just what is a college—how does a college differ from a dormitory?

INTERVIEWER: Because of the special quality of the Yale system?

SAARINEN: Yes, it is based on the Oxford and Cambridge system of small groups living and working together, sharing their social life and education. As much as possible, all that should be part of this little college—in a sense, this little monastery— in which young people isolate themselves to a certain degree from the practical things of life, from the distractions on the outside, and are therefore able to concentrate more on their studies. The problem was: How does one create that kind of world in the present age?

INTERVIEWER: A medieval world, then, re-expressed in modern terms?

SAARINEN: Yes, obviously you want to *re*-express it; you don't want to copy. The spirit could have been gotten by just building some more Gothic dormitories there. You can't deny that the old buildings at Yale have a special flavor, and to certain people the only reason for not copying them is that we can't afford it—they would cost so much more today. But the problem is much deeper and much more interesting. Even if we could afford it, we wouldn't want to repeat because we want to be part of our own time. The terribly difficult thing about Yale was that there was no answer to the problem within the vocabulary of modern architecture; so one really had to find a new vocabulary for this special problem. I also felt that existing modern materials had no answer to it, and we had to take that into consideration.

INTERVIEWER: Isn't there a place for traditional materials in modern architecture?

SAARINEN: Are you asking just where do stone, brick, concrete, or wood fit in modern architecture? Now those are materials which can be used beautifully, and often have to be in terms of surroundings. But if one is to put his most rational coat on, I think one would say that metal and concrete are really the only two materials of our time—concrete really has two expressions: one, poured in place, as in our cantilevered building in Milwaukee, and two, precast, as in our Oslo embassy (page 81). The handiwork of brick doesn't seem quite the right thing in relation to the whole building process today, nor does the craftsman's stonework. In a way, we can't get as much out of stone as we used to.

INTERVIEWER: What about your new American embassy in London (page 81), where you *did* use stone?

SAARINEN: All right, take London. There the site was most demanding because Grosvenor Square is basically a neo-Georgian pattern and those are permanent surroundings. The general mass, the general scale, was dictated by all this. Now the program and planning of the building were not essentially different from those of any other embassy—it was only a larger embassy. Nor was the planning much different from any office building as such. But the third part of the problem—the spirit—was very different. What should this building have, we asked, which the ordinary office building doesn't have? This is a government building; it ought to have some kind of Federal spirit. It also should have a spirit of being in London. So I went around London a great deal to see how the Portland stone weathered. I saw how London is basically black and white, and how all the public buildings are made out of just that stone and how really beautiful it is, but beautiful only in a quite broken-up façade. Only then does the weathering become nice on that stone. A plain façade, such as the Time-Life Building in London, becomes bleak and ugly, with soot running down from the window sills. So we decided to use Portland stone in a broken-up façade.

INTERVIEWER: In spite of what you said earlier about stone not being so impressive a material today as it was in the past?

SAARINEN: Well, at first we thought of a concrete façade which would express the precast concrete structural system. Would it not have been purer to do as we had in Oslo, not to cover it with stone but to leave the structural elements exposed? There we used emerald-green Norwegian granite as the surface concrete aggregate. We could have used Portland stone in a similar way. We could have built the structural members themselves right out of this so-called "reconstructed" Portland stone so that it would have been all one casting and the structural grille would not have been covered by an "old-fashioned" material like stone. This seemed a very desirable thing to do, but I spent a day looking at buildings of reconstructed Portland stone and found that they don't weather nicely. Fifty or even thirty years later, it is not so nice a material as the real Portland stone.

INTERVIEWER: Then the decision rested on the building's patina?

SAARINEN: One of the most important things about a building is how it ages. My father always said that either you use a material that ages well or one that ages not at all. Glass, for instance, does not age at all. I decided that it was better to cover the structural members with Portland stone. Every project has many modifying factors and many special problems.

INTERVIEWER: Do the solutions to each of the special problems finally add up to an over-all solution?

SAARINEN: You start by thinking of them separately, and then somewhere along the line you start putting them together in the structural system. If everything goes ideally, the structural system reinforces the inevitable solution to the site problem, while at the same time the inevitable solution to the programing and planning problem helps solve the problem of the spirit.

Saarinen's design for the Jefferson arch in St. Louis: a parabola of stainless steel.

INTERVIEWER: Can we say that the spirit is part of the total function of a building, superseding its merely practical function?

SAARINEN: I like to use the word "function" only in relation to programing and planning; if you include the spirit as part of the function, then you just open the barn door and anything goes. The Brown Derby restaurant, for instance: its shape has a function.

INTERVIEWER: What of a building that has primarily a spiritual function, such as your Jefferson National Expansion Memorial arch in St. Louis (above)?

SAARINEN: You are really saying that the spirit is the function of the Jefferson arch. Before one had the spirit one certainly didn't have the program, and there was no need to consider square-footage and so forth. You had the site and the spirit; out of those came the program, and the structural system was the thing that locked them in place.

INTERVIEWER: How did the site affect the design of the memorial?

SAARINEN: There again, the first things to think about were the Mississippi River, the levee, the surrounding buildings that eventually will be developed, Eads Bridge, and the other side of the Mississippi. One had to envision this whole as one great bowl and consider what kind of monument seemed right for that. Now before I had actually seen the site, I had thought that some kind of open vaulted structure would be a very nice monument—like the Pantheon, but maybe the Pantheon in lacework of some kind. This really was before Bucky Fuller and his geodesic domes, but I envisioned something like that until it became obvious that such a form wouldn't work on that site.

INTERVIEWER: Why not?

SAARINEN: Because it is a long, long site, facing the river. To place a round thing there would be to lose all relationship with the river. It would not rise up from the levee; and in accordance with the spirit of the problem, I was trying to reach for an absolutely permanent form—a high form. Stainless steel would seem to be the most permanent of the materials we have, and it seemed the thing one could trust most. I wanted a high form because the function of the whole thing, a commemoration, suggested the Washington Monument—which, incidentally, I think is a marvelous monument to Lincoln, just as the Lincoln Memorial in spirit is the right kind for Washington. But that's beside the point.

INTERVIEWER: I don't think so, if we're discussing a monument as important as this one is—and if you're not joking.

SAARINEN: No, I feel that. You know, Lincoln was a lone person, much more than Washington, who was a person of a different kind of era.

INTERVIEWER: What about the Jefferson Memorial in Washington?

SAARINEN: Well, you know, it's not so good as the others. But the basic shape does not seem wrong for Jefferson. In a way, it's the same as our Jefferson Monument in St.

TEXT CONTINUED ON PAGE 82

1
2
3
5
TWA

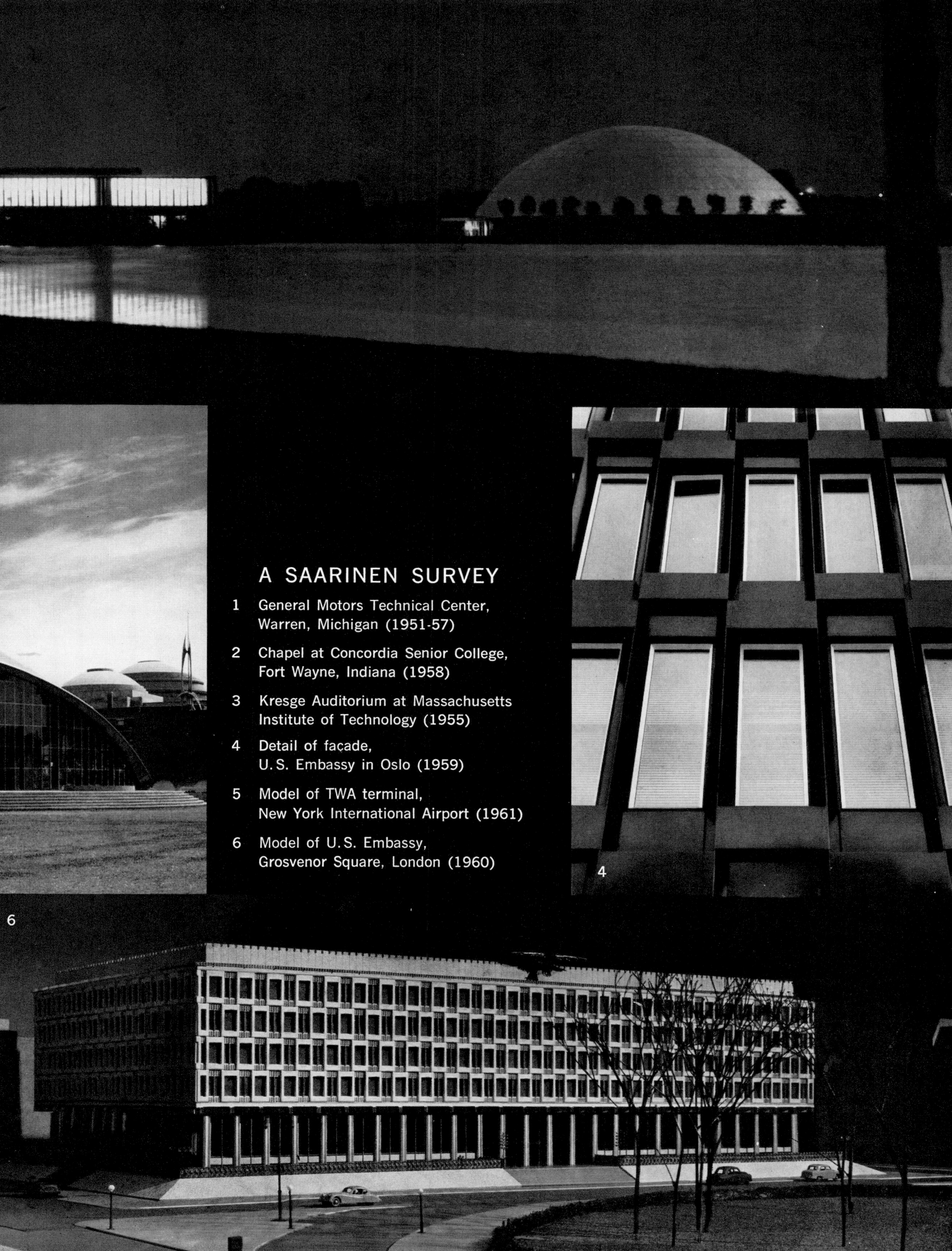

A SAARINEN SURVEY

1 General Motors Technical Center, Warren, Michigan (1951-57)

2 Chapel at Concordia Senior College, Fort Wayne, Indiana (1958)

3 Kresge Auditorium at Massachusetts Institute of Technology (1955)

4 Detail of façade, U.S. Embassy in Oslo (1959)

5 Model of TWA terminal, New York International Airport (1961)

6 Model of U.S. Embassy, Grosvenor Square, London (1960)

4

6

TEXT CONTINUED FROM PAGE 79

Louis—in one case the dome, in the other case the rounded arch. I was thinking of the problem in that way, and only later did it occur to me that it was a gateway to the West.

INTERVIEWER: What about your new TWA terminal at Idlewild (page 80), which has been compared to a bird in flight? Was there any intentional symbolism there?

SAARINEN: Let me go back a little to explain. A few years ago we did the M.I.T. auditorium (pages 80–81), theoretically a very graceful building. It has a very thin shell. Structurally, it's quite a rational building. But, if you look at it, isn't it a little bit too earthbound? The movement, the inevitable movement of an arch form, seemed to be downward: it did not have the soaring quality or sense of lightness that one wanted. Maybe it even has a certain heaviness. We wanted to counteract the downward gravity pull of the vault, and that we tried to do in TWA. In other words, we wanted an uplift. The fact that to some people it resembled a bird was really coincidental. That was the last thing we thought about. People are forever looking for literary explanations. I like much better the story I was told about the goalie on the Yale hockey team who said, after playing in our new rink, "Now I understand what all those professors mean about architectural expression. When I look up at that arch, I feel 'Go, go, go!'"

INTERVIEWER: Would you say you were trying to create dynamic space in TWA the way Baroque architects did?

SAARINEN: That's right, the Baroque architects were wrestling with the same problem. Within the limitations of the classical order, they were trying to see how far they could go into a nonstatic architecture. At TWA we tried to take the discipline imposed by the concrete shell vault and give it this nonstatic quality. We were doing the same thing, but using different play blocks.

INTERVIEWER: Then structural efficiency is not the only factor you consider when developing a purely modern form such as a concrete shell?

SAARINEN: In a way we are talking about the same thing as Vitruvius when he said that architecture consists of "commodity, firmness, and delight." The spirit of a building is related to delight, planning to commodity, structure and materials to firmness. I think what Vitruvius meant is that firmness is more than engineering. To me the Gothic is the greatest example of that. It was great engineering, but at the same time great form, great detail, great technology, great scale, great everything.

INTERVIEWER: I've noticed that, rather than depending on drawings, you give exceptional importance to working models and even to full-scale mock-ups of certain details of your buildings. Is this to get a better "feel" of the structure? And if it is, how is the experiment working out?

SAARINEN: So far it has been very successful and necessary. If Renaissance architects drew a façade, they could then imagine it completely. If they put in some shadows, they could see the whole thing; and since the material was stone, there was no problem in visualizing the three dimensions. But many of our projects involve completely new vocabularies which are impossible to see in drawings. I do not have the imagination Wright had—an absolutely unbelievable three-dimensional imagination. But even he got into trouble by not making enough working models. In the new Guggenheim Museum in New York there are many corners that might have been resolved better had those rooms been done first in model form.

INTERVIEWER: You have often expressed admiration for Wright. What do you think will be considered his most significant contribution to the modern movement?

SAARINEN: Wright was the greatest architect of his time, but I've always felt that he is very misunderstood. Many people have been influenced by him, but influenced by his personal form, not by his great concept of architecture. I think more time is needed so that we can get further away from him, and then he will be more fully understood. He saw the building whole, as one organism, and he saw that organism in relation to its surroundings. He did not conceive structure separately: his structure, his funny decorations, his spaces, his lighting, were all one thing. Today we have all this "icky" kind of architecture which is taken a little bit from here and a little from there. Go around a corner and it's a Corbusier thing here, a Wright thing there.

INTERVIEWER: How does Le Corbusier rank with Wright?

SAARINEN: Let's say that Wright is the Michelangelo and Corbu the Leonardo da Vinci of our time. But on this question of making the whole thing one, you can ask about Corbu's building at Marseilles—*is* it all one thing? Would Wright have put those peculiar sculptural forms on the roof the way Corbu did, or would he have integrated them with the total mass? I think Wright would have integrated it more. Corbu separates things, but they are held together by this terrific inventive spirit. Just how, I haven't quite figured out—but they are.

INTERVIEWER: We've mentioned two modern masters. What of Mies van der Rohe?

SAARINEN: I'm a great admirer of Mies. The influence of his Illinois Tech—his wonderful logic and structural clarity—can be seen in our General Motors Technical Center; a very strong influence.

INTERVIEWER: But the mood of the General Motors Tech Center (pages 80–81) is very different from that of Illinois Tech.

SAARINEN: There are so many things in General Motors that I owe to my father. He was still alive and we were partners at the time when the general site planning was done, although I can take most of the credit, I think, for the design. But the placing of buildings, their relation to one another, the use of water, the ribbon of color going through the whole project—so many things—all go back to my father. There is much similarity between Cranbrook and General Motors—I mean similarity in principle not in form. The problem at G.M. was essentially one of creating a unified environment, so you would know you hadn't gone across the street and were looking at someone else's buildings.

INTERVIEWER: Would you say that the problem of unity is the main difficulty facing planners today?

SAARINEN: We can learn from the experience of a university, which in a sense is a permanent environment, whereas so much of the American city is not. At the University of Chicago there is one small court, whose four different sides were done by four different firms about 1920 or so. They were among the best firms of their time, and they were all building in Gothic. They all had the discipline, larger than themselves, of the Gothic. But if you took four architects today and asked them to build the four sides of a quadrangle, the result would probably look like hell. We haven't developed that kind of over-all discipline.

INTERVIEWER: Especially in urban design.

SAARINEN: Some terrible mistakes are being made. We have these tremendous redevelopment projects, well financed, scientifically planned. They all look very good on paper. Then you see them when they are up, and you wonder whether they are really

CONTINUED ON PAGE 123

Saarinen's multilevel terminal for the new jet airport outside Washington will have its roof slung from two rows of concrete piers (pictured above). But its chief innovation will be the mobile lounges shown at the rear of the terminal in the cutaway drawing below. Larger and more luxurious than buses, they will be used to carry passengers between the terminal and their planes.

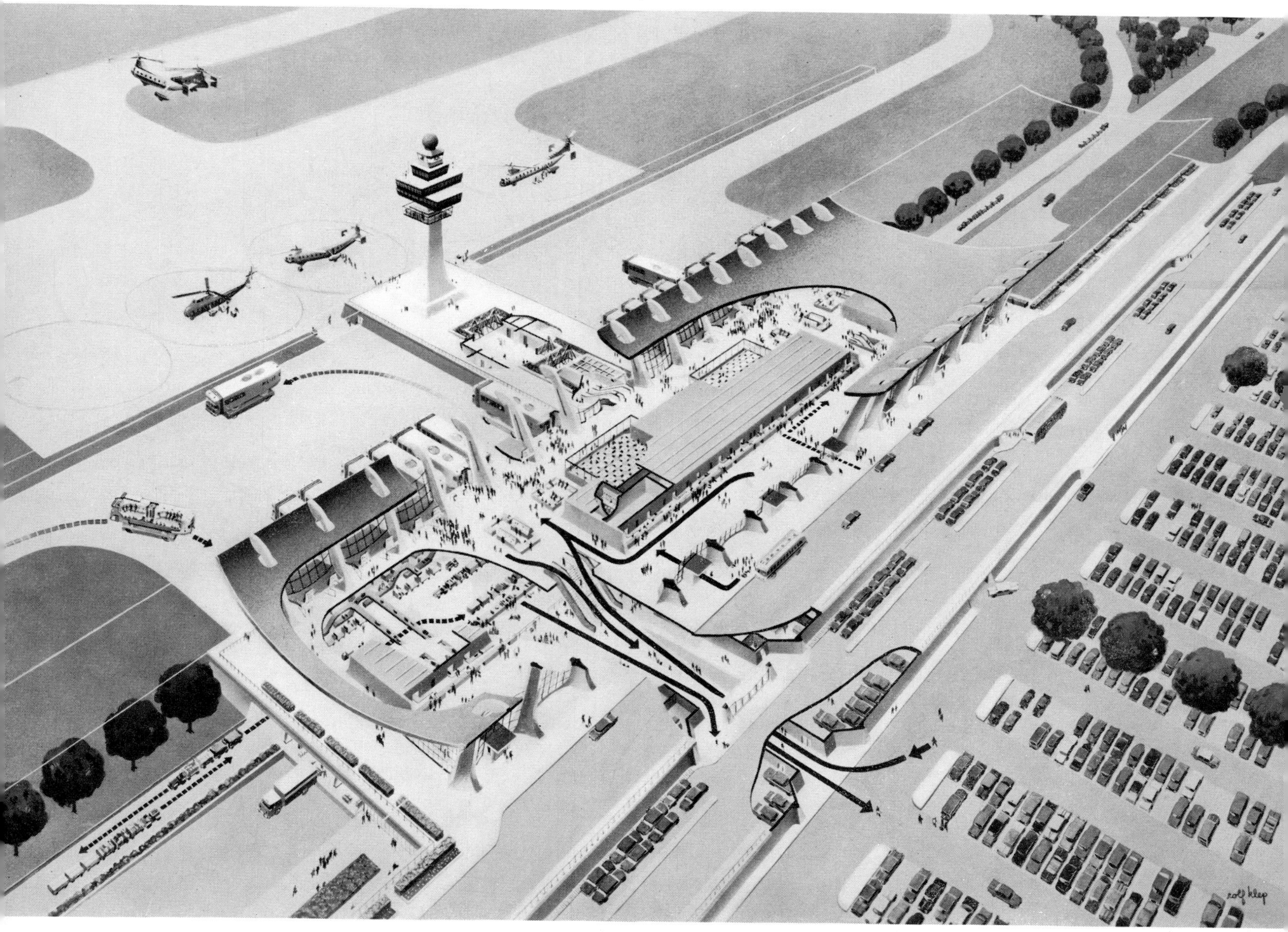

FROM *Histoire de la Marine*, L'ILLUSTRATION, PARIS 1942

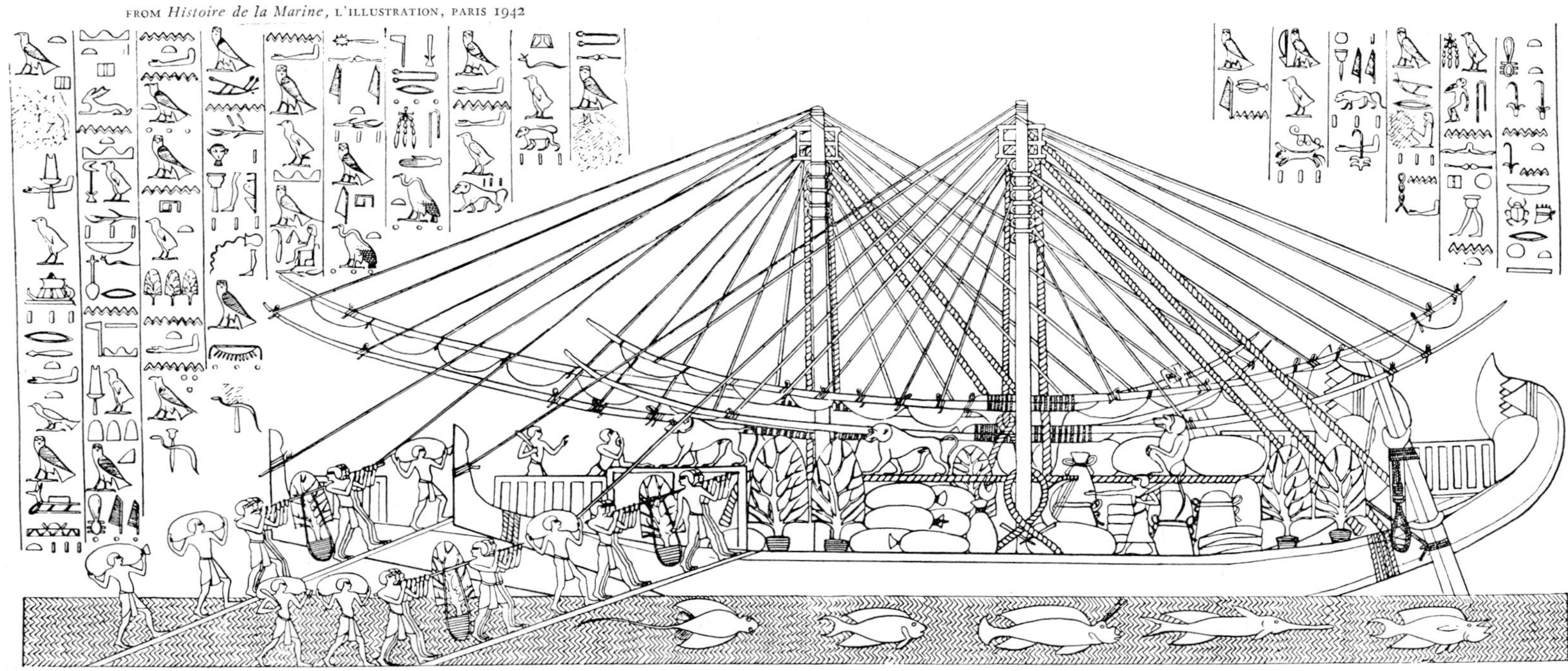

An Egyptian ship of the Eighteenth Dynasty loads a cargo of rare flora and unchained baboons from Punt, in this relief from Queen Hatshepsut's temple at Deir el-Bahri.

Man's most daring explorations today are directed not around but away from the planet on which we live. If we are on the threshold of entry into outer space, we are equally at the end of a period of discovery of the earth itself. The voyages of earthly discovery covered vast spaces, and only now do we realize how far back many of these reach in time. For archaeological finds made in very recent years tell a dramatic story of early adventure reaching far beyond what had long been regarded as the ultimate human horizons of those days. Enough evidence is now in hand to show, in fact, that explorers and adventurers in prehistoric eras reached out farther than many of their successors in the chronicle of recorded time.

The later stages of discovery are well known to us. Looking back through the centuries, from the nineteenth to the thirteenth, we see the known world shrinking steadily as our eyes pass Livingstone, Cook, Magellan, Columbus, Vasco da Gama. Peering back beyond Marco Polo, we see the horizons closing in upon Europe and the southern shores of the Mediterranean. When we think of the world at the time of the Crusades, we see only this small area lighted up, known and traversed; beyond it lie the dark regions of *terra incognita*.

For the inhabitants of that area at that time, the picture was true; that was the way they looked upon their world. For us, of course, this view is parochial in the extreme. There were other lighted areas. The Arabs occupied one that stretched from Transoxiana and the region of Bombay to Morocco. The Chinese knew the world from Ceylon to Japan. The Polynesians were getting a fair grasp of the layout of the Pacific. But it is true of all these areas that they were patches of light in a world mainly dark, that the unknown was vastly greater than the known, and that the fringe regions were the abodes of mermaids, rocs, and sea serpents, of fabulous riches and fabulous dangers.

As we go further back in time, the darkness closes in even more. To the north there is a brief flash, Vinland the Good, found and then lost again. But otherwise there is a gradual and regular diminution in the area of the known world. Oddly enough, the fall of Rome did not affect this historic movement. A larger area was known and traversed in the depth of the Dark Ages than at the height of the Roman Empire. About A.D. 1100 a guidebook was published in Iceland giving the best routes for travelers to Constantinople and Jerusalem; about A.D. 500 the golden horns of Denmark bore

Although it was long thought that Western man's explorations began with Jason's legendary voyage, archaeologists now find that in a still earlier millennium, Mediterranean traders journeyed as far as India and Sweden with such goods as ivory, amber, and bronze

BEFORE THE ARGO

By GEOFFREY BIBBY

pictures of the New Year festival in Constantinople. Yet only four centuries before, in A.D. 100, Scotland had been unknown territory to the Romans.

Four hundred years earlier, in 325 B.C., there was another flash of illumination when the Greeks, under Alexander, reached the Indian Ocean. But backwards from Alexander the darkness closes in rapidly. Herodotus, describing the known world, scarcely got beyond Egypt and the nearer frontiers of Bulgaria and Persia (although a Greek physician at the Persian court, writing about 500 B.C., had given an account of Persia and India for Greek readers). And Homer, singing in 900 B.C. or thereabouts of events then three hundred years in the past, clearly regarded his heroes as venturing into the fabulous fringe areas if they sailed outside a triangle bounded by the Dardanelles, Crete, and the western islands of Greece.

The bard cannot be accused of a parochial outlook. A few centuries after Homer, Ashurbanipal, ruler of Assyria, the greatest power of the time, wrote of an embassy from Gyges, the king of Lydia, as coming from "a district across the sea, a remote place, of which the kings, my fathers preceding me, had not heard the mention of the name." Yet Nineveh was no farther distant from Lydia than Chicago is from New York.

It would seem that in going back further we are nearing the beginning of things, that another century or so will take us to a time when the world that lay over the hill or around the headland from a man's own village was the Great Unknown, when the whole world showed nothing but feeble sparks of light, each invisible to the next.

Certainly the Greeks of Homer's time believed that the period before the Trojan War (by the archaeologist's reckoning, say 1300 B.C.) was just such an era of isolation. The legends of the time are full of stories of kings' sons—Jason, Oedipus, Theseus—banished or carried off as children to be brought up in the next parish, apparently without the news ever crossing the hill. Tales of long voyages survive from that period, that of the Argonauts being the most detailed, but the Argonauts were clearly portrayed as having no idea where they were going. They sailed in the general direction in which the ram with the Golden Fleece had flown a generation before, and by the time they reached the Dardanelles, they were in the mythical lands of nymphs and magic wells.

So there, it would seem, we have the whole story: a continuous expansion of man's knowledge of his world, com-

BRITISH INFORMATION SERVICE

Evidence of contacts between the Aegean and northen civilizations during the Bronze Age has been found at Stonehenge, England. Dagger carvings on one of the sarsen stones (below) resemble the bronze blade found in excavations at Mycenae (right).

ALISON FRANTZ FOR THE MYCENAE EXCAVATIONS

R. J. C. ATKINSON, UNIVERSITY COLLEGE, CARDIFF

mencing about 1000 B.C. and progressing over a period of three millennia, from complete darkness to complete light—a satisfying background before the onward leap to the stars.

And yet—what came before? The Greeks were satisfied to begin the history of exploration—and indeed all history—with the Argonauts. There *was* no history before Jason and his generation, the warriors of the Age of Bronze, when, as Hesiod wrote, "armor was of bronze and tools were of bronze; for black iron was not yet." Go further back and you come to the Ages of Silver and of Gold, said Hesiod, the time of the Noble Savages, nameless and innocent and content.

But today we cannot be content with this. We who are preparing to explore space have already for a hundred years and more been engaged in the exploration of time, and the simple answers no longer suffice. While Livingstone was following the Zambezi River, Rawlinson was deciphering the cuneiform script of the Babylonians, even as Champollion had learned to read the hieroglyphs of the ancient Egyptians. With the later unraveling of the Sumerian, the Hittite, and, most recently, the Urartean languages, and the "Linear B" script of Crete and Mycenae, written history has become available to us from a period of slightly more than a thousand years before ever the *Argo* sailed. And written history has been checked, supplemented, confirmed or disproved, and illustrated by the work of the archaeologist, while his diggings, his potsherds and stratifications, his pollen analysis and radioactive carbon dating have brought within the definition of history the actions and movements of men and of peoples in regions and in eras that no ancient writing, deciphered or undeciphered, has ever described. Using this new evidence, what can we say of man's knowledge of his world during the centuries and millennia that preceded the three thousand years of ever-widening horizons which led from the *Argo* to the moon rocket?

If the apparent ignorance shown by the contemporaries of Homer and Ashurbanipal of the world beyond their horizon leads us to expect the people of the preceding thousand years or so to have been preoccupied with digging their own cabbage patch and happily ignorant of their neighbor's patch, we are due for a series of surprises.

In Mesopotamia, and in particular at Ur of the Chaldees, in graves which can be dated to about 2500 B.C., there have been found sixteen round soapstone seals such as were used to sign or mark cuneiform tablets. But these are of a peculiar character; they are not the usual cylinder-type seal used generally during that period in Mesopotamia. Forty seals of the same type have recently been found on a little island off the Kuwait coast, a little way down the Persian Gulf; 225 similar seals have been found on Bahrein Island, 250 miles farther south by east; and three more have been unearthed from the ruins of Mohenjo-Daro, one of the two cities of the enigmatic Indus valley civilization in faraway Pakistan. Moreover, some of the Mesopotamian seals are inscribed in the still undeciphered script that was current on the banks of the Indus. The conclusion is inescapable that well over a thousand years before the *Argo* sailed for Colchis, Indus valley merchants were in the habit of sailing to Mesopotamia, or that Sumerian merchants voyaged to India, or both.

The seals are not the only evidence. In the temples of Ur, clay tablets from this period have been discovered that are, in effect, bills of lading, lists of cargo carried by ships chartered for trading voyages to the island of Bahrein, 350 miles away. The return cargo lists show that, at Bahrein, the ships took on freight coming from a land far off to the east known as Meluhha. And these cargoes included such characteristic Indian treasure as ivory, gold, and carnelian.

In Eridu, not far from Ur, were found two clay tablets inscribed about 1400 B.C., which proved on decipherment to be file copies of letters sent by a trading house of that city to its agents on Bahrein. The letters confirm the booking of a passage for a lady passenger and complain of the delay in shipment of a cargo of dates. The one extraordinary thing about them is their date.

At Deir el-Bahri, in Upper Egypt, stands the magnificent temple-tomb of Queen Hatshepsut, who ruled Egypt from 1502 to 1480 B.C. Its walls are covered with hieroglyphs and paintings depicting the most important events of her reign. And to judge by the space given to it, not the least important of her exploits, in her own eyes, was the dispatch of a successful expedition to a land she calls Punt. There has been much speculation among the learned as to the precise location of Punt. Identification is made more difficult by the fact that the ancient Egyptians themselves were clearly in no doubt as to where Punt lay. Accordingly, they included no directions for reaching it. All we know of the route thither is that it was by sea, beyond the Bab el Mandeb, the southern gate of the Red Sea. There is every reason to believe that Punt lay in Africa; Somaliland, Kenya, and points south have all been suggested as locations. The vegetation and animal life of Punt was African; we know this because the expedition recorded in the temple carvings was manifestly a scientific one, sent out to bring back specimens of the flora and fauna of Punt for the botanical and zoological gardens of the Pharaoh.

From the centuries immediately before 2000 B.C., a remarkable series of monuments have survived along the coasts of Europe. Throughout the islands and along the shores of the Mediterranean, they take the form of large communal tomb chambers, built in courses of stone, topped by a domed roof and approached by a long passageway, the whole covered by a mound of earth or stones. Along the Atlantic coasts, in Spain and Portugal, northwestern France, western England, Ireland, the Western Isles of Scotland and the Orkneys, north Germany and Denmark, and south Norway and Sweden, precisely the same type of burial chamber and mound is found, to the number of several thousands. But in these countries they are built of massive upright stones, capped by equally massive roof slabs. The resemblance between these

TEXT CONTINUED ON PAGE 90

PHOTOGRAPHS DR. CARL SCHUSTER

The labyrinth motif, originating in the eastern Mediterranean in the early Bronze Age, turned up a few hundred years later as a traditional design on a Cretan coin (above) and on the Etruscan Tragliatella vase (right). Its appearance in Ireland, on the famous Hollywood stone (below), indicates an active sea trade between the Mediterranean and Atlantic countries during the Bronze Age.

NORTH SEA
BALTIC SEA
DVINA
NEMAN
VISTULA
ODER
ELBE
WESER
RHINE
SEINE
LOIRE
DANUBE
DNIEPER
DNIESTER
BLACK
ATLANTIC OCEAN
ADRIATIC SEA
AEGEAN SEA
MYCENAE
CRETE
MEDITERRANEAN SEA
NILE

PREHISTORIC TRADE ROUTES

The passage-grave builders traveled from the eastern Mediterranean as far north as Scandinavia. Their route by sea was west to the Atlantic and by land through France. Perhaps, through these same paths, the image of a Mycenaean dagger found its way to Stonehenge, England. The Beaker People spread east from Spain, and their bell-shaped vessels have been found in England and across the European land routes to Poland. Faïence beads, common to Egypt and Mesopotamia, have been found in these same areas and even farther east to Siberia and as far south as Central Africa. Danish amber was transported down the rivers of Europe and reached Britain and Crete by the sea path which was opened by the passage-grave builders. The round soapstone seals of the Indus valley found at Bahrein and Ur tell of a flourishing trade on the Persian Gulf.

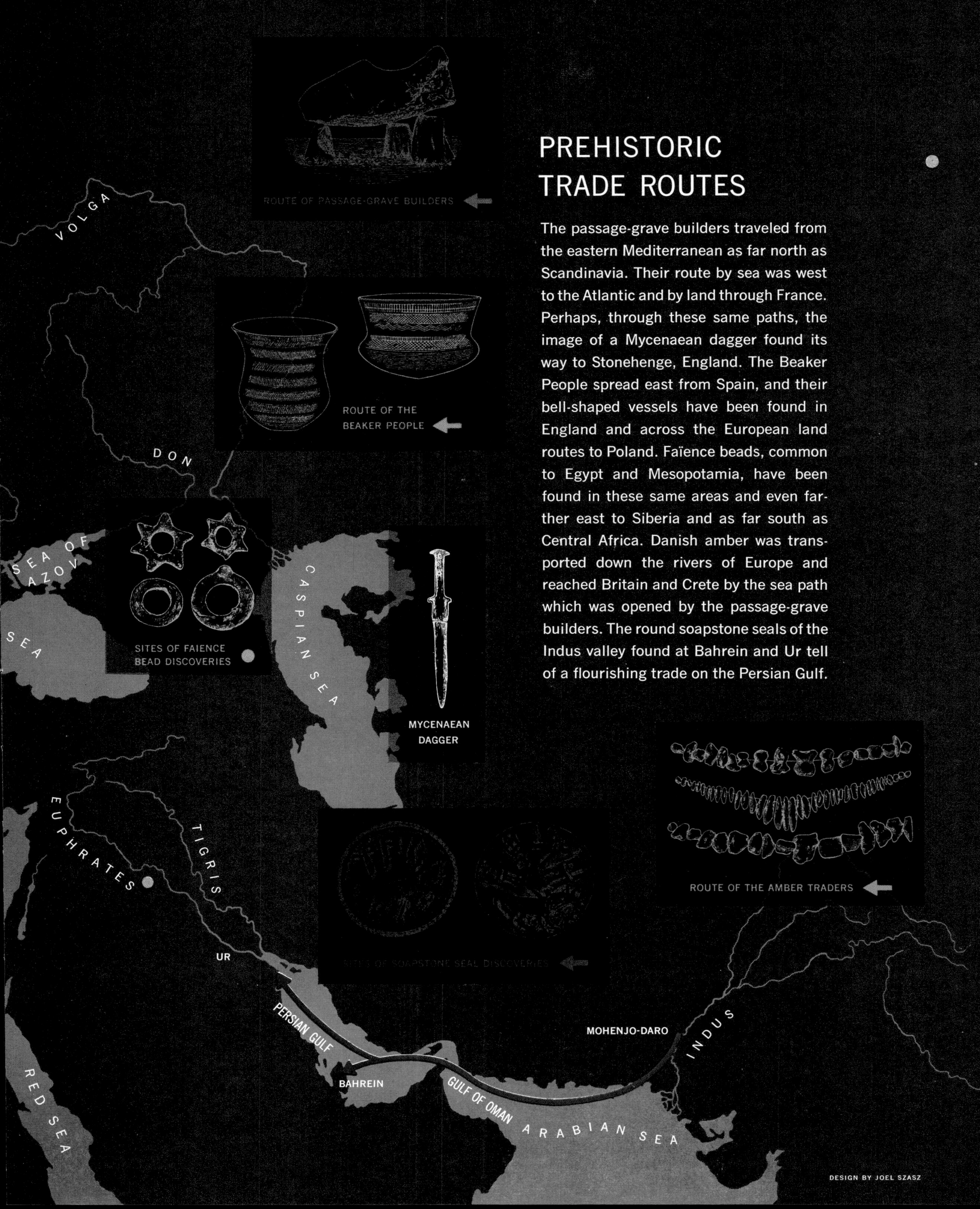

ROUTE OF PASSAGE-GRAVE BUILDERS

ROUTE OF THE BEAKER PEOPLE

SITES OF FAIENCE BEAD DISCOVERIES

MYCENAEAN DAGGER

ROUTE OF THE AMBER TRADERS

SITES OF SOAPSTONE SEAL DISCOVERIES

VOLGA

DON

SEA OF AZOV

SEA

CASPIAN SEA

EUPHRATES

TIGRIS

UR

PERSIAN GULF

BAHREIN

GULF OF OMAN

MOHENJO-DARO

INDUS

ARABIAN SEA

RED SEA

DESIGN BY JOEL SZASZ

TEXT CONTINUED FROM PAGE 87

passage graves, scattered along five thousand miles of coastline within a span of at most two hundred years, is so close that no prehistorian has ventured to doubt that they are related to each other—the outward signs of some community of interest along the shores of Europe four thousand years ago. There is little reason to doubt that they are the visible evidence of a religion, or at least of a common belief in existence after death, which began in the eastern Mediterranean about 2400 B.C. and was spread by small bands of men who traveled by sea westward and northward around Europe in the course of the next two centuries. Certain it is that the passage graves are rarely found more than a day's journey from the sea, except where, as at the Pyrenees, an isthmus can be crossed from sea to sea.

The Beaker movement is a different proposition in every way, though equally significant from our point of view. Built some two hundred years after the passage graves, the small burial mounds of the Beaker people are found dotted thinly over Europe, from Spain to Poland and from Italy to Ireland. In England they are very numerous, bearing witness to an occupation of the country by Beaker folk, but elsewhere they are sparse intrusions among the regular inhabitants. Everywhere the artifacts buried in these graves are identical: bronze daggers, barbed arrowheads, archers' wrist guards, large buttons of jet or amber—and beakers. These bell-shaped drinking vessels have given their name to the people who used them, and their shape and ornament are so uniform, wherever the Beaker folk are found, that one is tempted to think of mass production.

Where the passage-grave builders traveled by sea, the Beaker people traveled by land, spreading out, it would appear, from Spain in small parties over the length and breadth of Europe. That they were archers is clear. The fact that, with their coming, bronze implements and ornaments first appear among populations that previously used only flint suggests that the Beaker people's primary concern was bronze-trading and tinkering.

There is other evidence of early trade in Europe, and again the distances are vast. The primary sources of amber in Europe are the Baltic and the North Sea coasts of Denmark. During the late Stone Age in northern Europe, from about 2600 to 1600 B.C., amber was exceedingly common. Huge necklaces, comprising hundreds of amber beads, and buttons as large as a clenched fist have been found in graves and the ruins of settlements. But with the onset of the Bronze Age, about 1600 B.C., the amount of amber placed in graves diminished sharply. At the same time amber began to appear in the Near East. Clearly trade was in operation here, and discoveries along the Elbe and the Oder show that at least some of the trade routes followed the rivers running north and south across Europe. But the discovery of identical gold-mounted amber ornaments in Crete and in Britain suggests that other routes followed the seaways around the coasts of Europe, the routes opened up by the passage-grave people. And the discovery of carvings, on the sarsens of Stonehenge, of a dagger and axes that resemble the types used about 1500 B.C. by the Mycenaeans of Greece, suggests that visitors, perhaps architects, had come to southern England from the eastern Mediterranean at the time when Stonehenge was erected in its present form.

The occurrence of faïence beads tells an even clearer story. Faïence, a fused and glazed quartz, was the first type of glass ever made. As early as 4000 B.C. it was used for small figurines and beads in Mesopotamia and in Egypt, and for the next two thousand years and more it was confined to the eastern Mediterranean, to Mesopotamia, and to the Indus valley. But about 1500 B.C. the picture changes. Around this time faïence beads, particularly of a star-shaped and a segmented variety, appeared over a truly vast area. They have been found in large numbers in England, on the trans-European trade routes, in France, Czechoslovakia, and Poland, as far north as Scandinavia, as far south as Kenya in central Africa, and as far east as Siberia. All are of the same type, and clearly they are not of local manufacture. They are the clearest possible evidence of trade emanating from Egypt, or thereabouts, and following partly the sea route around the coasts of Europe and partly the river routes across Africa, Asia, and Europe.

This abundant evidence of trade by land and sea in the years between 2500 and 1500 B.C. has an interesting corollary in the far north. On the smooth slabs of the rock outcrops to the east of Oslo Fiord, in southern Norway and central Sweden, the people of the Bronze Age, about 1500 B.C., suddenly developed the custom of carving pictures. It is agreed that these pictures are mainly portrayals of religious festivals and sacred symbols, but even so they give a variegated picture of the life of the times. Here we find pictures of ritual plowing with teams of oxen, representations of oxcarts, horses, and chariots. But one subject predominates: seafaring. Over and over again are portrayed ships, ships singly and in huge fleets, ships with high prows and sterns, ships with sails and with oars, up to twenty oars a side. There can be little doubt that these people of the coastal regions of Scandinavia, at the time of the *Argo* or a little before, were seamen first and only secondarily farmers. The ships portrayed are no small vessels designed for coastal travel; they are as large as the vessels which, two thousand years later, regularly sailed from the same region to Iceland, Greenland, and the coasts of Maine.

These, then, are some of the factors which we must take into account in any assessment of man's knowledge of his world in the days before the Argonauts. They add up to a broad picture very different from that which the early Greek writers and the chronicles of the later Assyrian and Egyptian kings might have led us to expect. Apparently, from about the middle of the Third Millennium to about the middle of the Second Millennium B.C., a very large area of the world was continuously known and traversed. The civilized portion

The men of Punt arrived in the Egyptian city of Thebes bringing a tribute of incense-bearing trees, ostrich eggs, feathered fans, and beads to the King's newly appointed vizier, Rekh-Mi-Re. Their presence at this celebration during the Eighteenth Dynasty proves the two-way traffic that existed between Egypt and this almost mythical land, "on which no others have set foot." This painting from the tomb of Rekh-Mi-Re in Thebes shows these Puntites from the southern coast of the Red Sea as a racial mixture of dark-skinned Hamites and Negroes.

of the world was small, comprising little more than Greece, Crete and Asia Minor, Egypt and Palestine, Syria and Mesopotamia. But from this circumscribed area traders, missionaries, and, perhaps, even casual tourists went out, journeying over incredible distances, and doing this so habitually that there can be no doubt that the traffic was regular, safe —and profitable.

Nor must we imagine a one-way traffic from the Near East to savage lands below the horizon. We have seen the evidence for Indian merchants in Mesopotamia and for amber export from the "perimeter" to the Mediterranean. There were large ocean-going fleets based in Norway and Sweden, and it may well be that not only was the trade reciprocal—as trade must always be—but that much of it was in the hands of seamen and shipowners from the "fringe" areas. Trade was not entirely radial—that is, outward from and inward to the Near East. The Beaker folk sent their caravans across the direction of the main trade routes, from one peripheral area to others, while Irish gold in Scandinavia and Scandinavian

CONTINUED ON PAGE 113

On Stage: GEORGE C. SCOTT

Quite apart from his technical array of talents, which are of a breadth and depth equaled among his contemporaries only by Christopher Plummer and Jason Robards, Jr., George C. Scott is very likely the most theatrical figure to bestride the American stage—something he seems to do even when sitting down—since John Barrymore was seen in *Hamlet* and *The Jest.* In a theater pretty much committed to the conscientious deprecation of externals, Scott is an anachronism, a bravura performer whose style is as exuberantly chiseled as a Byzantine capital. A producer and director for whom he has worked speaks of his "absolute presence."

For Scott, the process of making his presence felt on stage is, while artistically sound, currently heretical; it is the antithesis of the fashionable Broadway-Stanislavsky Method (with which there is nothing organically wrong save that some actors, sweating humorlessly to get inside themselves before getting out, occasionally carry it to peaks of brooding foolishness). "I don't see any point," Scott says, "in squeezing dry a piece of work for days before it's even on its feet in rehearsal. It's like taking a five-month fetus out of the womb and shaking it." He switches metaphors in mid-exposition: "I let the play get hold of me and we are both swept along together." He switches again: "There are lights and shadows. Some become clearer tomorrow, some the next day, some a week after that, and finally the whole premise begins to light up."

During the Broadway theatrical season just ended (which Brooks Atkinson called the worst in memory), Scott provided one brilliant note—as the Judge Advocate of *The Andersonville Trial.* In the New York *Times,* Atkinson wrote of Scott's performance that he "develops a diabolical affection for his victim," the commandant of the infamous Confederate prison. Scott achieved the effect by putting an arm tenderly about the man whose execution he must demand, at the same time bestowing on him a smile of hatred very nearly palpable.

Scott's major film role has also been as a prosecutor—in *Anatomy of a Murder.* Here, too, his graceful bearing, his sibilant and quiet delivery conveyed the same sense of terror that an onlooker might feel in watching a tiger stalk an unsuspecting victim.

A couple of seasons ago, Scott made his first Broadway appearance opposite Judith Anderson, herself a noted externalist, in *Comes a Day.* He played a murderous psychopath. One scene called upon him to crack his knuckles, a piece of business usually requiring two hands. Since childhood, however, Scott, whose hands are powerful but otherwise unremarkable, has been able to produce the sound with either one. He suggested he be allowed to play the scene that way, and night after night audiences watched the grotesque tour de force (Scott favored his left hand) in stunned fascination.

In an unconventional way, Scott at thirty-two is a handsome man, even a romantic-looking one, and therefore better suited than a good many other actors to work the way he does. He is six feet tall and quite slender but very strong. (Scott is a native of Wise, Virginia, a strip-mining coal town. He once worked as a common laborer for a brother-in-law, a building contractor, and he spent four years in the Marines.) His face is saturnine, thin, and oddly crescent-shaped, a shape not unlike those stylized, archaic representations of the quarter moon to be found on calendars; the mouth is broad and well defined under an even broader nose which is not so well defined after having been broken a number of times in barroom brawls and left unrepaired. (Scott is an arrested alcoholic and bears his cross, if not exactly with equanimity, at least laconically.)

Although he is irrevocably committed to the theater, Scott is not certain he wants to be an actor all his life. He would like eventually to produce and direct, possibly to write. (He was a journalism major at the University of Missouri, but quit within a few points of a degree.) It is clear that he is at once drawn to acting and repelled by it. "Actors are forever concerned with themselves," he says, "with their bodies, their loves and hates. When you think of having to sift and absorb all of the things a play must have, channel them through the nervous system and blood stream, and then expel them at a given target, it is bound to have an effect on the machine. Early in his career, an actor is fortunate. He can be a hundred different people and it is a kind of therapy for him. Later, it is simply a form of desperate escape from himself.

"Then, you are dealing," he says, speaking of audiences, "with people you love and despise at the same time. One has to woo them, conquer them, make them think and be moved. They are like virgins. But every night there is a whole new set of virgins. After a while, you become some sort of Don Juan always looking for this great, monstrous kind of love."

GILBERT MILLSTEIN

Photograph by EUGENE COOK

On Stage: COLLEEN DEWHURST

Late this winter, thirteen or so years after making her professional debut in a yearning but slapdash stock company in Gatlinburg, Tennessee, Miss Colleen Dewhurst, a thirty-six-year-old actress of singularly opulent talents, played her first leading role on Broadway. Her long wait in the wings was a further proof of the American commercial theater's celebrated discomfort in the presence of, so to speak, the unclassifiable. Her vehicle—the late Albert Camus's *Caligula*, in which she played Caesonia, mistress to Kenneth Haigh's paranoid emperor—closed after just thirty-eight performances; yet it helped secure a fame already established off Broadway.

Miss Dewhurst, who bears a striking resemblance to the Aubrey Beardsley drawings of the noted French actress Réjane, in particular to his portrait of her as Madame Sans-Gêne, is quite beautiful in the classical manner—tall, wide-browed, long-eyed, straight-nosed, deep-chested, broad-hipped, and regal of carriage. Her movements are correspondingly luxuriant, as is her voice. The quick general impression she gives—apart from her ability—is an overpowering one, lying somewhere between an army with banners and a Las Vegas stripper with a college education (two years of which Miss Dewhurst received at a school called Milwaukee-Downer).

In terms of today's uniform, natural-shoulder casting, here is a difficult proposition with which to deal. She has neither the unblinking, tiny charm of the ingénue nor the homogenized surface éclat of the conventional leading lady, and she is far too handsome to play character parts. What finally may have stopped many Broadway producers magnetized by Miss Dewhurst is alarm at her rampant vitality and natural power of attraction, which are slightly larger than life as it is customarily lived on the American stage. Actresses of her kind do well in Europe, in repertory or not. In this country, by and large, they go off Broadway. (If they are outstanding performers, they may work regularly in television and less regularly in motion pictures as second-leading ladies, villainesses, or betrayed wives.) When they come to Broadway, it is invariably in the kind of play described as "offbeat," one which could just as well have been put on away from Times Square, except that it is usually the work of a distinguished foreigner and therefore, although highly intellectual, may just break even.

Such was the case with *Caligula*. Between the summer of 1956 and 1958, Colleen Dewhurst was seen off-Broadway in *The Taming of the Shrew, Titus Andronicus, Camille,* Cocteau's *The Eagle Has Two Heads, Macbeth,* and Edwin Justus Mayer's *Children of Darkness,* making her appearance with such notable groups as the New York Summer Shakespeare Festival and Circle in the Square. Most off-Broadway of all, she appeared in *A Moon for the Misbegotten,* in Spoleto, Italy. Her notices were very nearly unanimously favorable. It is characteristic that two of her most important television successes were in "The Play of the Week" on New York's Channel 13: in *Medea*, as the first lady of Corinth to Judith Anderson's Medea, and in John Steinbeck's poetic fantasy, *Burning Bright,* which had been a failure on Broadway.

On the basis of her career thus far, and despite what others have found her to be—"stargazer," "dream-walker," and "child of nature"—there is reason to believe that Miss Dewhurst is something like the person she says she is. (The simple facts: She was born in Montreal, an only child; her mother, a Christian Science practitioner, is dead; her father, once an outstanding athlete who made a pretty fair one of his daughter, is the sales manager of a lighting concern in the Middle West. Miss Dewhurst has been married and divorced.)

"I find myself doing a thing I cannot help," she says. "If I read for the part of a certain kind of woman and find that I like her, why, then we can cross the stage, meet, and merge; if I don't, there's no point in my playing her. No one's going to get anything out of it. I have had attached to me a word: strength. What is strength? I *do* like things large and I like them passionate. This is a big, passionate world. There's no fight between passion and bravura and realistic acting, none at all."

"I don't see the theater in terms of self-aggrandizement," she goes on, "or self-aggrandizement as a goal. If that were all, simply to get the better role, then there would be a terrible zero in my life. I've looked myself in the face. However angry, slobbering, wolfish, or ugly my inner devil is, I will not push it down and say, 'You do not exist.' No, I believe it's up to me to exorcise it somehow, not in ignorance either, not by telling myself, 'I am good, I am good, I am a treasure, I am a joy,' but by obtaining some crucial knowledge of myself as part of a whole. Then if I can reach inside myself, with the idea of bringing out some kind of beauty, some kind of joy, then I will be able to get across something about life itself."

GILBERT MILLSTEIN

Photograph by EUGENE COOK

Rapallo right side up

PHOTOGRAPHS BY ART KANE

RAPALLO'S REFLECTIONS

Since the time Rapallo on the Italian Riviera was sacked by the Turks and Barbary pirates during the sixteenth century, its chief invaders have been literary persons who have swarmed there in numbers since the Edwardian era (the best-loved luminary being Max Beerbohm, the most fought-over, Ezra Pound). Today's travel guides warn that "writers seem to lurk behind every tree" (Fodor) and that the place is "blatant," a "typically crowded, second-rate oasis" (Fielding).

Perhaps mindful of this disdain, the American photographer Art Kane stood beside a canal in Rapallo one day in summer, wondering how to record his visit, when his eye was attracted by shimmering reflections of objects and people in the clear, slow-moving water. "I have been obsessed with reflections for years," says Kane, "shooting them in puddles, windows, mirrors—any kind of shiny surface." So he pointed his camera not at town and people but at their reverse images in water. First he shot a reflection of houses (left), then of a couple on a bridge (opposite). But Kane, formerly a painter, was most captivated when a rowboat with two men approached, and he shot the sequence of four reflections shown on the next pages. To convey the fresh, painterly qualities he found in mirroring familiar subjects, HORIZON presents his prints turned upside down.

By M. I. FINLEY

WAS SOCRATES GUILTY AS CHARGED?

History and myth, echoing Plato, have answered No—but his fellow Athenians had compelling reasons for saying Yes

"This indictment and affidavit are sworn to by Meletus, the son of Meletus of the deme Pitthos, against Socrates, the son of Sophroniscus of the deme Alopece. Socrates is guilty of not believing in the gods in which the city believes, and of introducing other new divinities. He is also guilty of corrupting the young. The penalty proposed is death."

When Socrates, then seventy years old, was put on trial in his native Athens in 399 B.C., the proceedings began with the clerk of the court reading this indictment aloud to the large (but normal-sized) jury of 501 men, all citizens in good standing over the age of thirty. The Athenian system of government was amateur in the strict sense of the word: there were no district attorneys, scarcely any police, and no professional lawyers. If a crime was committed, major or minor, some individual—acting in a private capacity—had to do something about it. He had to lay a charge before the proper official, as Meletus did, and then he had to attend the trial, mount the rostrum, and present his case to the jury. Meletus was supported by two other men, Anytus and Lycon. When they had taken their allotted time, controlled by a water clock, it was Socrates's turn. He denied the charges, defended his life's work and his ideas, and by direct interrogation challenged Meletus to produce the young men whose religious beliefs he had corrupted.

This took hours, while the jury sat on their wooden benches and the spectators stood about behind them. As soon as the speeches were finished, the verdict was given.

COURTESY METROPOLITAN MUSEUM OF ART—WOLFE FUND 1931

Philosopher to the end, Socrates calmly reaches for the hemlock in J. L. David's somewhat melodramatic painting (1787)

Athenian juries, unlike their modern counterparts, had full control of the decision. They were judge and jury together, and there was no appeal from their verdict. Nor did they have an opportunity to discuss the case. They simply filed up one by one and dropped their ballots into an urn. The votes were counted in sight of everyone, and the result was announced immediately: guilty 281, not guilty 220.

When a defendant was convicted, the jury had next to fix the penalty, which they did by voting once more, this time on choices put to them by the accuser and the defendant. Meletus asked for the death penalty. In reply, Socrates seems to have made a series of frivolous counterproposals; for example, he suggested that he be voted one of the highest honors the state could confer, namely, maintenance at public expense in the Prytaneum for the rest of his life. This behavior was so offensive that, if the ancient evidence is to be trusted, eighty of the jurors now switched their votes, and the majority for capital punishment was a large one, 361 to 140. Socrates then went off to jail and everyone else went home, each juror receiving as pay for the day's work three obols, half a workman's normal wage. A month later Socrates drank the cup of hemlock, having refused his friends' efforts to persuade him to flee the country, and died quickly and painlessly.

This much about the trial of Socrates is clear and straightforward enough. But very little else is, and that is a pity. Socrates and Athenian democracy are both dead, but his trial remains alive as a great myth, and like all myths, it is believed—by those who believe it—to exemplify a universal truth. Here is the proof, it is said, of the tyranny of the majority, of the trampling of the voice of reason and individual conscience by mass rule, of the common man's hatred of the man of genius. Socrates may be dead, but the issues are not. That is why it is still important to know what facts lie behind the myth.

The prime, although not the only, source of the myth is an early work of Plato's known as the *Apology*. (The Greek word *apologia* means "defense"; it does not imply that a wrong has been done for which the wrongdoer begs pardon.) This book appeared a few years after the trial and pretends to be the actual text of Socrates's two speeches to the jurors. It is necessary to say at once that it was nothing of the kind. All the proceedings in Greek trials were oral. There were no stenographers, and no official records were kept other than the text of the indictment and the verdict. No one could later report the speeches in full unless the speakers themselves had written them out beforehand and preserved them. This Socrates surely had not done. Instead, the *Apology* is a brilliantly dramatic piece in which Plato's hand is visible in every paragraph. In addition, we have two other accounts of Socrates's trial, both by Xenophon (still others were extant in antiquity but are now lost). These versions do not agree with each other, and in places they are quite contradictory.

Here before our eyes is the mythmaking process at work. These "apologies" could be written and circulated precisely because there was no authentic text of what Socrates really said. In fact, Plato himself hints elsewhere that, far from making the great speeches of the *Apology*, Socrates gave a bumbling performance. He was no orator but an arguer and conversationalist; what was very effective in small groups of disciples was of no use, and even harmed his case, in a set speech to a large, partly hostile, and inattentive audience. It is doubtful that this mattered much in the actual event: most Athenians had had thirty or forty years to make up their minds about Socrates, and no single speech was likely to have changed anyone's mind in 399 B.C., any more than today. But the death of Socrates mattered very much indeed to his disciples, so much so that they wrote the "apologies" which, in their view, Socrates *should* have made. That is to say, they took a stand on the issues, on the politics and morals of the Athenians—which they disliked violently—and on the teaching of Socrates and the meaning of his life. Plato's view of these things was not Xenophon's. Because Plato was by far the greater man and the more persuasive, his view prevails down to our own day. And yet, that is not necessarily proof that he was right.

Paradoxically, it is not what Socrates said which is so important, but what Meletus and Anytus and Lycon said, what they thought, what they were getting at, and what they feared. To begin with, who were they that they should initiate so vital an action? Unfortunately, we do not know anything of consequence about either Meletus or Lycon, but Anytus was a prominent and responsible political figure, with a career of considerable distinction and patriotic service behind him. His participation creates a strong presumption that the prosecution was a carefully thought through step, not a merely frivolous or petty persecution.

And who were the jurors who decided that Socrates must die for what he taught? Every year in Athens there was drawn up a jury panel of 6,000 men, volunteers for the service. For each trial, the requisite number was selected from the panel by lot. Since in 399 B.C. there could not have been more than 20,000 men all told who were eligible to sit on juries, Socrates was tried and condemned by a sizable percentage of his fellow citizens. We know nothing about them individually, but granting that there may have been a disproportionate number of the very poor, who wanted the three obols; of the very old, who found jury duty an entertaining and exciting way to pass the time (at least that is what the comic playwright Aristophanes alleged in *Wasps*); and of the richer men, who could afford to give time to their civic duties, the 501 jurors were not a bad sampling of the citizenry. Judging from that sample, the conclusion is that the Athenians were divided about Socrates. More correctly, they were divided on the question of how dangerous he was, for many of those who were willing to acquit thought him either a fool or a bore, or both.

Obviously we cannot know what went on in the minds of individual jurors while they listened to Socrates and his accusers. We cannot say why each man voted as he did. But we do know a lot about their collective experience. The most important fact in their lives was the great war between Athens and Sparta, the Peloponnesian War, which began in 431 B.C. and did not end (though it was interrupted by periods of uneasy peace) until 404, five years before the trial. In 431 Athens was the greatest power in the Greek world, head of a very considerable empire, prosperous, and proud—proud of its position, of its culture, and, above all, of its democratic system. "The school of Hellas" it was called by Pericles, and Athenians believed and cherished that claim. By 404 everything was gone: the empire, the glory, and the democracy. In their place stood a Spartan garrison and a dictatorship (which came to be known as the Thirty Tyrants). The psychological blow was incalculable, and there was not a man on the jury in 399 who could have forgotten it.

Nor could they have forgotten the appalling losses of the war. Two great plagues struck the city almost at the beginning, and in the four years 430–426 they carried off about one-third of the population. In 413 Athens made an all-out effort in an invasion of Sicily. That ended in disaster: perhaps half the effective fighting force was killed or missing. Finally, the Thirty Tyrants butchered another 1,500 men, drove many others into exile, and plundered wealthy foreigners for their own personal enrichment.

It is testimony to the vigor of Athenian society that the city recovered as rapidly and completely as it did. The Thirty Tyrants had a short life: they were driven out in 403 by the combined efforts of a handful of the exiles and the survivors at home. The traditional democracy was then re-established, not to be challenged again for a century. One of its first actions was to declare a general amnesty, and so powerful was the spirit of conciliation that both Plato and Aristotle, of all people, praised the democratic leaders for it. "It is no wonder," Plato wrote in a letter, "that in this revolutionary period some people took personal revenge against enemies, but in general the restored democratic party behaved justly and equitably."

In Athenian trials each juror was given a pair of disks—perforated for condemnation, solid for acquittal—and cast his vote by dropping one or the other into a bronze urn.

AMERICAN SCHOOL OF CLASSICAL STUDIES, ATHENS

Nevertheless, it is a common view today that Socrates was tried and executed as an act of political vengeance by the restored democracy. It is true that Socrates was no friend of democracy as it was practiced in Athens. He criticized it freely and frequently, but on the other hand, he was deeply attached to Athens itself, fought in the hoplite ranks in several battles, and at least once in his life held office. There is nothing here to warrant the political vengeance theory, but there may be among his friends and disciples. One was Critias, the evil genius of the Thirty Tyrants, the most ruthless, brutal, and cynical of them all. Critias fell in the fighting that helped bring down the tyranny, and with him died Charmides, another of the Thirty. Charmides was uncle to Plato and well known as a disciple of Socrates. In these two men (and in others), we can understand easily enough how many jurors saw at work a poison which they traced back to the teaching of Socrates. Because of their bitter personal memories of the war and the tyranny, their votes may well have been turned, at least subconsciously, against a man who, they knew (and he himself never denied), had wrong ideas and even wronger disciples.

It is curious, however, that neither Plato nor Xenophon so much as hints at such a motivation behind the trial. They were both tireless opponents of democracy (Xenophon even fought against Athens on the Spartan side in 394 and went into exile, branded a traitor). How could they have missed this ready-made opportunity to demonstrate the wickedness of democratic rule? How could Plato have praised the spirit of amnesty which prevailed and go on, in the next sentence of his letter, to write, "By some chance, however, some of the men then in power brought my friend Socrates to trial"? When Plato said "by some chance" he meant just that and not "for political reasons." He was not so incompetent a writer; and I suggest that, despite what our textbooks say, Plato was right and political revenge will not do as an explanation, beyond its background role in the minds of some jurors. The simple fact is that the indictment accused Socrates of impiety and corruption of the young, and of nothing else. We live in an age which tends to be cynical about such matters: "It's all politics" is the usual comment. Maybe so, but the ancient Greeks took religion seriously on its own terms, and we must too, if we wish to understand the times.

To appreciate what an Athenian could have meant by "impiety" (the Greek word is *asebeia*), three facts must be kept in mind. One is that Greek religion had become very complicated over the centuries, with a great variety of gods and heroes who had numerous and crisscrossing functions and roles. The second is that their religion had little of what we should call dogma about it, but was largely a matter of ritual and myth. And the third is that it was thoroughly enmeshed with the family and the state. Impiety was, therefore, a very loose notion: a man could be deemed impious for desecrating an altar, for revealing the secrets of a mystery cult, or merely for saying things which were considered blasphemous. But whatever form an act of impiety took, the fundamental point was that it was a public matter: impiety was an offense not only against the gods but also against the community, and therefore punishment was not left to the gods but taken in hand by the state.

Because of the looseness and vagueness of the concept, its definition rested with the jury in each case. They decided whether or not a particular act, if proved, was punishable under the law. This meant in practice that the frequency of such charges and trials in Athens depended largely on the state of public opinion at any given moment. And the period of the Peloponnesian War was a bad moment. A decree was passed almost at the outset forbidding, as impious, the study of astronomy, very likely as a reaction—a typically irrational one—to the plague. The first victim was the great philosopher-scientist from Asia Minor, Anaxagoras, the friend of Pericles; and there were others. Simultaneously, as the cult of Asclepius, the magical healer, came to Athens and shot into popularity, oracle-mongers, diviners, and private soothsayers became rife in the city. In 415 B.C. there was the famous double sacrilege, the profanation of the mysteries at Eleusis and the mutilation of the hermae, which drove Alcibiades into exile (and others to their deaths) and may in consequence have cost Athens the war.

Against this background, Socrates was accused of a specific form of impiety; namely, that he disbelieved in the city's gods and introduced new ones. In Plato's *Apology* this is denied with great vigor, and there is sufficient and convincing proof that Socrates was in fact a man of very deep piety, who scrupulously performed the sacrifices and other rites. Besides, it is hard to see why the introduction of new gods should have been an indictable offense when it had been happening right and left just at that time. Not only had Asclepius arrived—he was at least a *Greek* god—but there was also an influx of foreign deities, like the Syrian Mother Goddess, whose shrines were set up with official permission. No one accused Socrates of joining in their worship, but even if he had, there could have been no objection. All that was said against him on this charge was that he was constantly referring to his inner *daemon*, which talked to him regularly and prevented him from taking wrong courses of action. This was more than the voice of conscience: Socrates plainly believed that it was a *god* who spoke to him. But in a society in which soothsaying was a recognized profession, that is pretty thin ground for prosecution.

There remains, then, the last and most crucial element in the charge: corruption of the young. Plato's *Apology* stresses (and justifies) Socrates's role as a teacher and allows Socrates to admit that his disciples were the young men with leisure for study—in other words, the sons of the wealthiest citizens. Of course Plato does not add that they came from precisely those circles from which the opposition to democracy was drawn, the Thirty Tyrants in particular. This was a fact known to everybody. Since there was no use in denying it, one could only try to ignore it and concentrate on the moral and religious sides of Socrates's instruction. In Xenophon's *Apology* there is a dramatic moment when Socrates turns to Meletus in court and challenges him: Name one man whom I corrupted from piety to impiety. Meletus answers: I can name those whom you persuaded to follow your authority rather than their parents'. Yes, replies Socrates, but that was a matter of education, in which one *should* turn to experts and not to kinsmen. To whom does one go when one requires a physician or general? To parents and brothers, or to qualified experts?

This interchange, fictitious as it no doubt is, somehow strikes at the heart of the issue. Until some fifty years before the trial, there was no Greek schooling to speak of. Children were taught to read and write and figure by the servants who looked after them, usually old male slaves. Beyond that level, formal instruction was restricted to two subjects, music and physical training. Men of the generation of Pericles and Sophocles learned everything else by living the life of active citizens: round the dinner table, at the theater during the great religious festivals, in the Agora, at meetings of the assembly—in short, from parents and elders, precisely as Meletus said they should.

Then, roughly in the middle of the fifth century, there came a revolution in education, especially at Athens. Professional teachers called Sophists appeared. They quickly attracted the young men of means to whom they gave higher education—in rhetoric, philosophy, and political science. A very good education it was, too, and at high fees. In the process they developed a startlingly new attitude among their disciples; namely, that morals, traditions, beliefs, and myths were not a fixed mass of doctrine to be handed on unchanged and without question from generation to generation, but that they were something to be analyzed and studied rationally and, if necessary, to be modified and rejected. Inevitably, these innovations were looked upon with great distaste and suspicion in many quarters. A kind of know-nothingism developed in reply. In one dialogue, the *Meno*, Plato satirizes this attitude with cold deliberation by making Anytus the spokesman of blind conservatism and traditionalism. "It is not the Sophists who are mad," he has Anytus say at the end, "but rather the young men who pay out their money, and those responsible for them. Worst of all are the cities who allow them in and do not expel them."

It is very much to be doubted that this is a fair portrayal of Anytus, but it surely represents a widely held view. Nor can we altogether dismiss it as the usual dislike some people always feel for anything newfangled. There was some of that present, to be sure, but there was also the fact that for a portion of the younger generation, liberation from rigid tradition meant unlimited freedom of self-assertion, unlimited rights, and no responsibilities except to themselves. One may speculate on how this conflict of values might have been resolved had the war not intervened. But the war did intervene. Then it was no laughing matter when young aristocrats organized a dining club called the *Kakodaimonistai* (literally, devil-worshipers), whose program was to mock at superstition. They tempted the gods, for example, by dining on unlucky days; and once, just as the Sicilian expedition had been well launched, the citizens of Athens awoke one morning to discover that in the night the sacred hermae which kept guard over streets and house entrances had been mutilated all over the city. If Anytus himself did not say that "worst of all" are the cities which do not expel the Sophists, we can be sure that many citizens did think and say that, or worse. There was a limit to how much blasphemy the gods would tolerate: when they had had enough, the whole city would suffer the consequences, not just the individual blasphemers. And so corruption of the young became, in the eyes of many, not a matter of abstract principle, but a practical danger to the city at a time when it was beset with troubles.

All this should have had nothing to do with Socrates. He was an inquirer and, in a way, a teacher, but he was not a Sophist. Indeed, he was their most bitter opponent. He objected to their teaching for pay, to what he considered their

CONTINUED ON PAGE 117

A Portfolio of Drawings by Morris Graves

CREATURES OF THE IRISH TWILIGHT

In 1954 Morris Graves came to live on one of the lonely finger-peninsulas of Ireland opening out onto the Atlantic. West Cork is not one of the obviously beautiful parts of Ireland: its subdued colors, drab grays and heather browns, do not flatter the mind. The decaying harbor village nearby is a cluster of stone buildings, gaunt as the beehive huts of an early monastic settlement. The sea merges with the eroding coastal land in the rock pools of a tidal river. A sparse but tender landscape, modified by the presence of man through long centuries.

Morris Graves came to Ireland as a refugee from the "machine-age noise" of life in Washington State. He took up residence in an isolated house appropriately called Inisbeg (Gaelic: little island). What he was looking for, he has described: quietude and the kind of concentration of nature he had known in the Alpine meadows of the Pacific Northwest, where clarity of atmosphere defines sounds of earth and air. What he found one can see in his series of drawings, some of which are reproduced here. In them, minuscule forlorn creatures of the Irish countryside, which haunt hedgerow, gleaming bog pool, and rough stone wall, are transformed into symbols of individuality. These are not the wild birds of the Pacific Northwest, combating primal forces and shaped by them: the obvious destructive element has been removed. One is reminded of the animals which turn the margins of the Book of Kells into an eccentric playground: pure intuitions of grace and fugitive loneliness.

In *Hedgerow Animal,* above, a land creature pursues a furtive errand of its own in the dusk. Nothing impinges upon its consciousness except the fulfilling of its errand and thus itself: the undulant line of doleful purpose from head to tail is the outer motion of its interior and determined integrity. The *Shorebirds* (overleaf), inhabitants of that marginal world where the elements of land and water meet, suggest a gregarious contrast. Ceaselessly in motion down the buffeting air, their flight creates a pattern within which each bird retains an almost spiky individuality.

The mournful *Seabird in the Rain,* with its black hermit's cowl, is as integral as the crepuscular animal on this page. Deluged in rain, he is not a creature of earth but of water, as much at home in his dour world as a mad monk in the light of withdrawn contemplation. And in *Hibernation, 1954,* the fourth drawing, Graves seems to dramatize this refuge aspect of Ireland which delights him: a sort of natural habit of introversion, both neurotic and spiritually fruitful. A solitary animal broods in his retreat, indwelling and turned as luminous as a pearl or an initial in a medieval manuscript. From and into its seclusion grows an incandescent envelope; dark and light, misfit spirit and removed secretive world blend.

The *Night Hedgerow Animal* of the last drawing seems to me the essence of the series. This lonely little figure, face screwed up intently, has its own misanthropic mind made up. Graves showed this drawing to a countryman in County Cork: "I can't name it but I've seen it meself," he said. It is the nature of this dwarf poltergeist to have the last word, even if, as seems likely, it be irreverent and nasty.

JOHN MONTAGUE

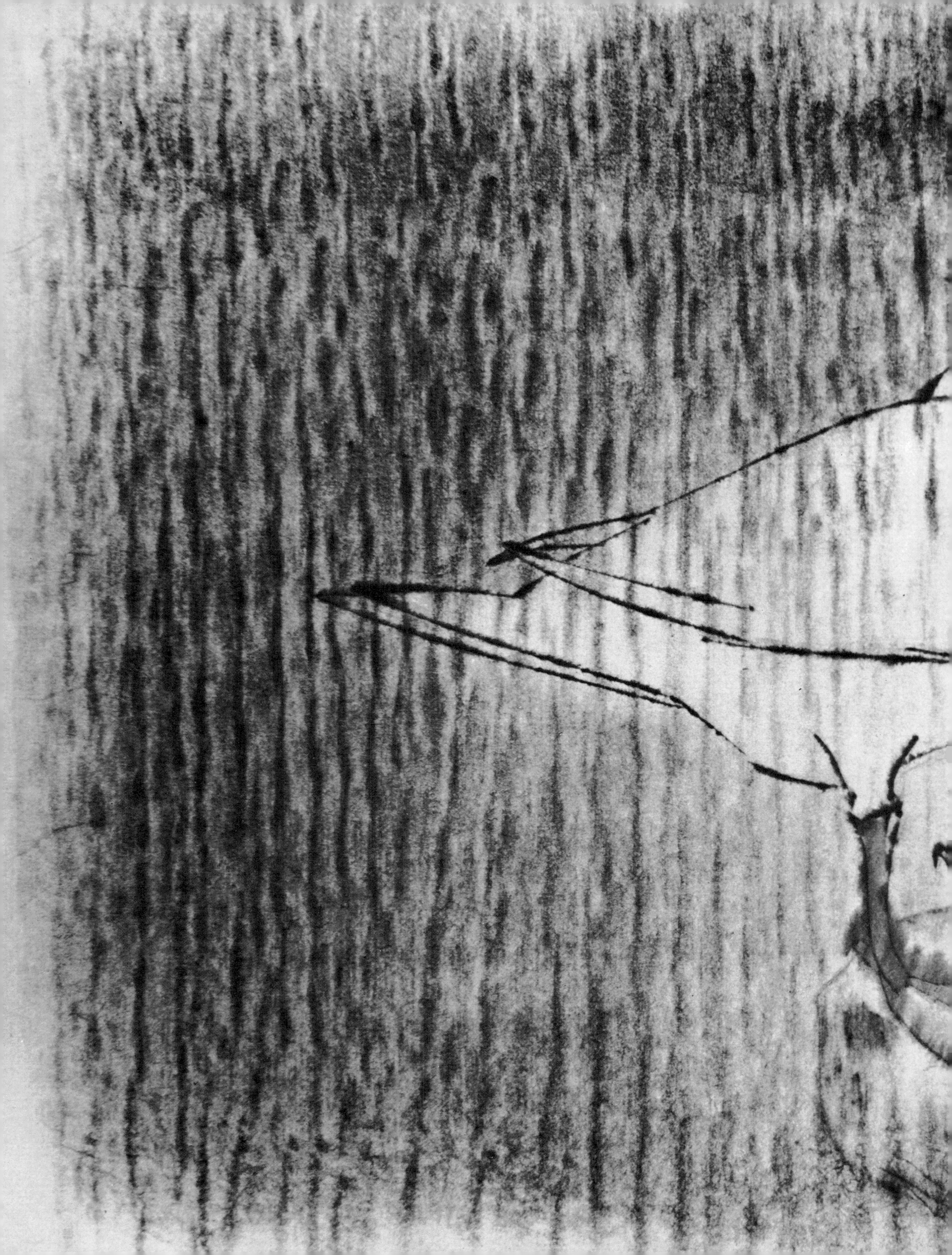

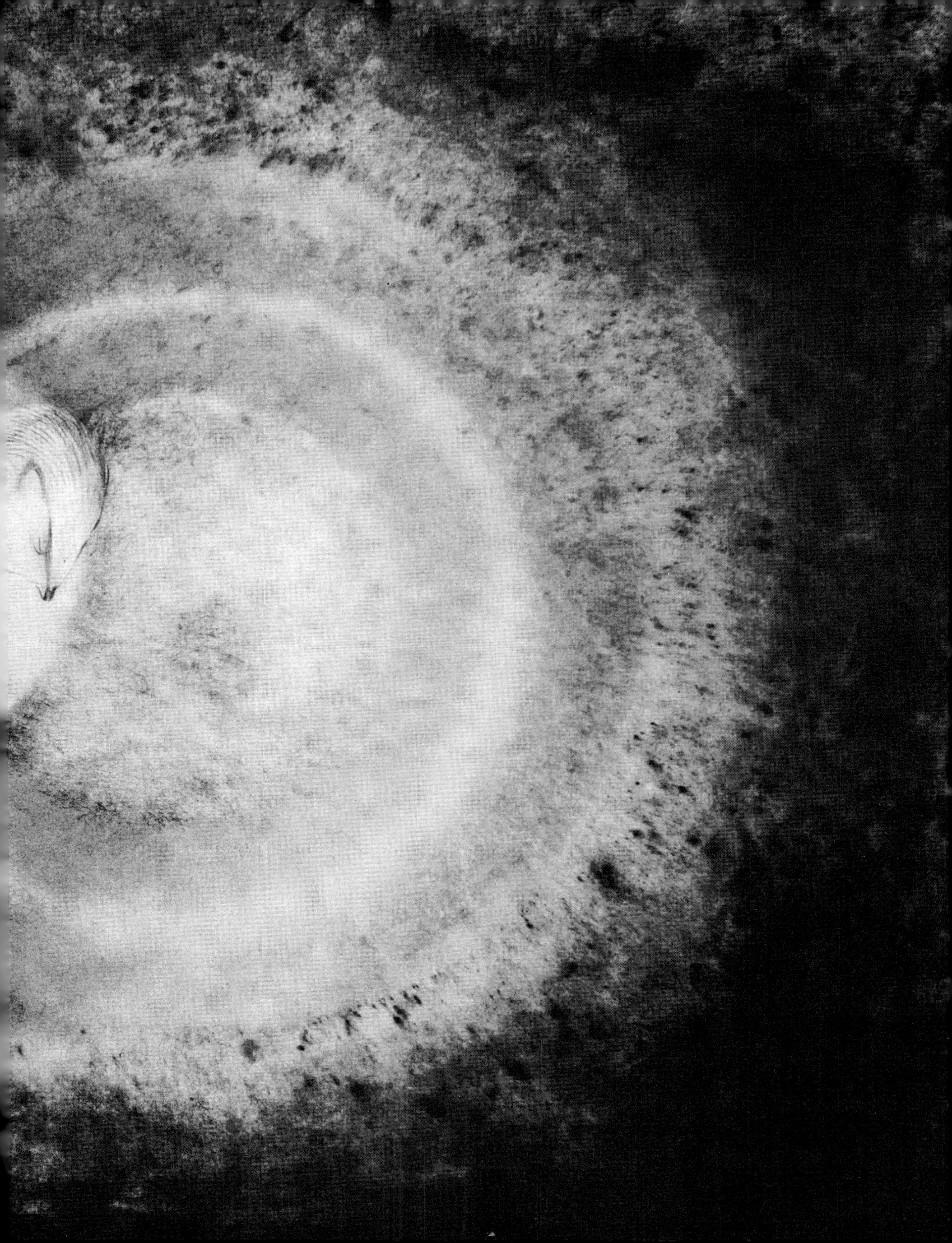

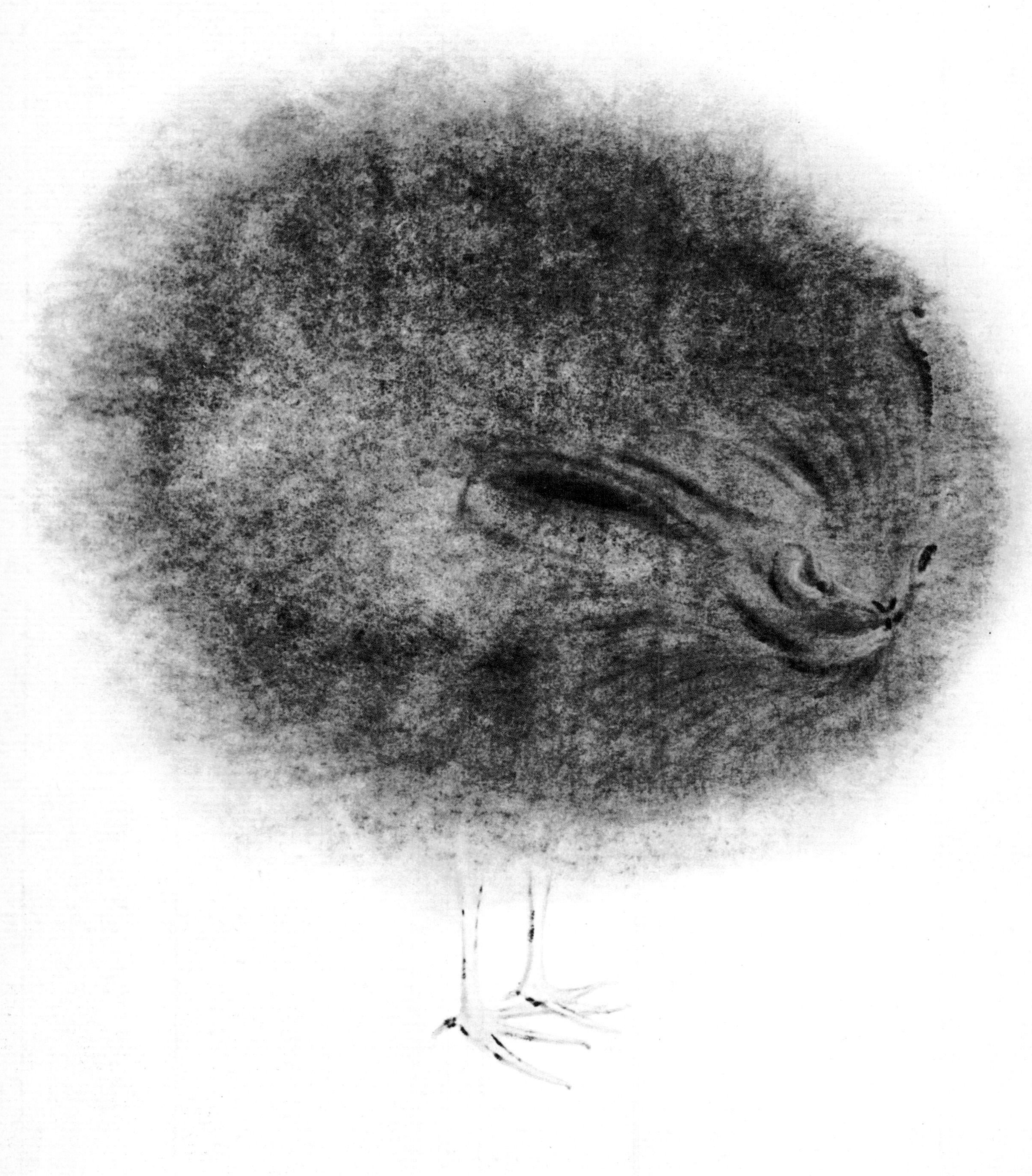

HEDGEROW ANIMAL, COURTESY DANNA JOHNSON; SHOREBIRDS, PHILADELPHIA MUSEUM OF ART, SAMUEL S. FLEISHER ART MEMORIAL COLLECTION; SEABIRD IN THE RAIN, COLLECTION OF WILLIAM S. ZIERLER; HIBERNATION, COLLECTION OF THE SARA ROBY FOUNDATION, N.Y.C.; NIGHT HEDGEROW ANIMAL, COLLECTION JOSEPH H. HIRSHHORN

BEFORE THE ARGO

CONTINUED FROM PAGE 91

amber in England and in Spain tell the same story.

Thus the picture is nearly filled in. From approximately 2500 B.C. to 1500 B.C. the whole world west of the Urals and the Ganges valley was an organized mercantile unity—and we have only negative evidence that the area of unity was not even larger.

What are the reasons for this? And, perhaps more important, why did the horizons of knowledge again narrow almost to the vanishing point by about 1000 B.C.?

The answer must be sought, partly at least, in the technology of the period. The period 2500–1500 B.C. was the height of the Middle Eastern Bronge Age and of the spread of bronze to the uttermost parts of Europe. Tools and weapons and ornaments were of bronze; the ubiquitous objects that literally hold a civilization together—nails and rivets and brooches and safety pins—were of bronze. The whole fabric of culture depended upon plentiful supplies of bronze. And bronze is an alloy of two comparatively rare metals, copper and tin. The search for and exploitation of these two metals is sufficient to explain the initial impetus to trade. And, once started, trade was self-perpetuating. The familiar pattern of reciprocal trading developed, raw materials moving in one direction and manufactured articles in the other. Manufactured articles, previously unknown and undemanded in the primary producing countries, became first luxuries and then necessities, and other raw materials, such as amber and jet and lapis lazuli, previously unknown in the manufacturing countries, were exported to pay for them. An expanding economy necessitated expanding markets, and the trade routes stretched ever farther.

And yet it ended. In the course of a few centuries, most of the world reverted to a subsistence economy, the trade routes dead and forgotten.

It would seem that what happened resulted from a combination of economic weaknesses, a technological innovation, widespread warfare, and, perhaps, climatic changes.

An expanding economy bears the seed of its own destruction, and its growth can be followed in the story of Bronze Age Denmark. Denmark was distant from the main centers of bronze manufacture and far from the trade lines of the Beaker bronzesmiths. Yet, from as early as 2400 B.C., the first copper and bronze articles, small ornaments such as rings and pendants, have survived in very small numbers from an otherwise purely Stone Age economy. Gradually, over the next eight hundred years, as the export of amber was organized, the number of imported bronzes increased, and they became more utilitarian; in addition to the ornaments, objects such as axes and daggers appeared in increasing numbers. But the economy was still essentially Stone Age, based on flint as the raw material for the tools of everyday life, and therefore basically self-sufficient. It was only about 1600 B.C. that bronze became the usual material for almost all tools and weapons and the Bronze Age proper began in Denmark. Bronze had ceased to be a luxury and had become a necessity.

But the corollary followed immediately. A country that exports raw materials and imports manufactured articles is vulnerable as soon as the manufactured articles become essential to its economy. Denmark rapidly established its own manufacture of bronzes, possibly aided by the equivalent of a preferential tariff system. Shortly, Danish bronzes were competing on the export market, not only in countries still farther distant from the original exporters but even in the countries lying between Denmark and the Near East.

It is probable that this growth of manufacturing industries in lands previously exploited as markets hastened regional self-sufficiency and, in consequence, the collapse of organized long-distance trade. But the process was aggravated by the spread of a new metal, iron. It was about 1400 B.C. that new smelting techniques produced the high temperatures which at last could produce an iron superior in strength to bronze. This development seems to have occurred in northeastern Turkey, and the process spread over Europe considerably more rapidly than had the art of processing bronze. Partly this was due to the fact that the spreading agency was war and the movements of peoples (which may in themselves have tended to disrupt trading relations), but chiefly it was because iron ore occurred more widely than copper or tin. Iron was in fact available for smelting in almost every land; it could even be extracted from peat bogs when there were no natural ore deposits. In effect, iron-forging offered every country the prospect of economic self-sufficiency.

It was eagerly seized upon—and the bottom fell out of the bronze market. Trade stagnated, ships were laid up, the recession set in. For a century or so the struggle went on, with competition more and more fierce for the contracting markets. Too literal a search for "the Trojan War's economic causes" has rightly been ridiculed, but commercial rivalry may well have acerbated the quarrel over the abducted queen. After the sack of Troy there were no more sailings to the world's end. But when Homer came to compose the stories of his country's heroic past, there were still traditions current of great ships which had sailed out to traffic for the riches of the lands below the horizon. If the *Argo* indeed existed, then its voyage must have been one of the last of the Bronze Age trading ventures, the end of the great period of exploration that preceded our own.

Geoffrey Bibby is a British archaeologist who heads the Department of Oriental Antiquities at the Prehistoric Museum of Aarhus, Denmark, and who wrote Testimony of the Spade.

FIGURES TO THE FORE

TEXT CONTINUED FROM PAGE 16

have been with some relief that they relinquished the burden of transcendental meanings and began to confront less unnerving subjects. As Diebenkorn says, "I came to mistrust my desire to explode the picture and supercharge it in some way." David Park put it another way when, explaining the subtle influence psychoanalysis has had on painting, he said, "It has helped establish a feeling that your faults have color, have value; so instead of working for perfection, you can work toward being yourself."

This new taste for simplicity and the human scale does not seem to be affecting the rest of vanguard American art. The mainstream of American and, in fact, world art is still abstract. And, in the last analysis, most of the advanced styles of the last thirty years are fundamentally intellectual: somewhere in back of almost all of them—dadaism or surrealism, futurism or nonobjectivism or abstract expressionism—is a manifesto or at least a theoretical platform providing a rallying point for the artists and a basis for public understanding. But manifestoes and aesthetic platforms mean little to the Berkeley trio. Amiable in his manner, Diebenkorn is nevertheless famous for evading theoretical discussion. Bischoff, kindly but reserved, is said to let go mainly when he is playing the horn in a jazz combo. "We're not the 'school of Pont-Aven,' " says David Park, most talkative and defensive of the three; "sure, we talk, but more in a nontheoretical, 'how's it gone today, kid?' type of way."

This relaxed attitude now pervades the lives and work of the San Francisco group and separates them from their colleagues on New York's Tenth Street by a distance as great as that from Middletown to Bohemia. Much less absorbed in the culture of their times than artists in the East, they "rarely" go to the theater (Bischoff), "don't know a thing about" science (Park), read "less on these topics [of aesthetics or art criticism] every year" (Diebenkorn). In David Riesman's term, they seem to be "inner directed." They work much more regularly than artists in the distracting metropolis. "I just paint," says Park. "I often get up early, about 7 o'clock, start painting, and paint until sunset at 8. Once every three months we go off for a vacation." "My working habits are regular," says Bischoff; "from 9 A.M. to 5 or 6 P.M. six days a week, with a half day of painting Sundays." They do not indulge in the colorful casualness of dress or home life which has marked vanguard artists since the middle of the nineteenth century. The populous suburban hills of Berkeley where they live are filled with large, natural-wood homes, liberally landscaped and overshadowed by eucalyptus trees. Houses crowd one another closely, yet behind his wooden fence or high hedge, the artist works at his own pace in the circle of his family. Park's grandchildren, he says, call him "old paint-head." The price of a sound house and of such emotional security comes high, so the three artists teach regular schedules: Bischoff at the California School of Fine Arts, Park at the University of California in Berkeley, Diebenkorn at the California College of Arts and Crafts in Oakland (though this may not be necessary much longer, now that they are selling their work in New York for substantial sums).

Although set apart from the "official" art world, these painters can hardly be said to represent a "California school" either. It is true that the colors they use are taken from the local landscape, though one may admit it (Diebenkorn: "I'm certain that this is a factor") and another deny it (Park: "I don't think so at all"). Yet in more important ways they seem to transcend a regional style, as Thomas Hart Benton and Grant Wood, for instance, never did. To begin with, regional qualities are hard to pin down in California. Undulant brown hills conflict with the craggy coastal rocks; placid days give way to seasons of rain; cloud banks pushing eastward like white slag are blown back to sea by an eerie, dry wind similar to the mistral, which brings the smell of the desert all the way to the coast. In the second place, if there is such a thing as a specifically Californian culture,* it is better expressed in the arts of potter and calligrapher, in open-plan houses and outdoor pavilions, and in the mildly moralizing poetry of Alan Watts and the Zen pacifists—most of them offshoots of the Orient. But in the art of Bischoff, Park, and Diebenkorn, there is a hard concern with form, which is related to Western painting much more than to the semi-Oriental style of, say, Mark Tobey.

If it is to the great Western tradition that one must look for sources or parallels to the San Francisco group, it is apparently to an earlier West than ours. Down along the west coast of Italy, south of Rome, in the rugged, variegated area called Campania, there flourished around the first century A.D. a society and an art of painting that suggest those in Berkeley today. It may be useful to compare those two otherwise disparate cultures. Then, as now, for instance, two artistic milieux beckoned: the metropolis (Rome/New York), with its great architectural projects, its laws and vital forces; and the countryside, where vacationers in rustic, open-plan villas bid for an art which was relaxed and suitable for leisurely contemplation.

Then, too, the very colors and geography of Campania are like those of California: stone meets sea in gigantic abutments, scrubby green foliage creeps across a gray and brown earth, the coast is bathed in sunlight reflected from a westward sea. As one might expect, this landscape, and the earth pigments available from it, gave rise to a scale of colors very much like those laid out today on the palettes in Berkeley—the brick reds, fresh greens, dark blues, and ivories one sees preserved in the National Museum at Naples.

Perhaps the most striking parallel is an aesthetic one: at

*See "The Flowering of San Francisco" by Allan Temko in HORIZON for January, 1959.

both these moments in history, one can point to a high ideal being brought down to a more human level. In Campania, of course, it was the old Athenian classical principle that the human body represented the order of the universe in microcosm; thus, art offered the same demonstration of universal truths as music, mathematics, and logic. In our time, it is the romantic principle that the artist, in his "divine madness," has the power to strike through surface appearances to the abstract essence of things—a principle expressed, among others, by Clyfford Still, whose theories continue to haunt San Francisco painting. However, by the first century A.D., some Roman artists had turned away from the heroic and godlike images of Athenian classicism and were trying instead to render an "illusion" of reality. Today Bischoff, Park, and Diebenkorn, turning away from Still's austere preoccupation with essences, have also come face to face with the problems of representing those "faults" in the construction of nature, those deviations from perfect order, by which the artist succeeds in suggesting reality to us. The way light is distorted as it falls through the air, the way the body is distorted by its baggage of feelings, the way the world is distorted by our eyes into relationships of scale and perspective —these are the very problems the vanguard Roman artist tackled. Each member of the Berkeley trio appears to have specialized in a single one of these problems and made it his real subject, to which the human figure is a useful accessory.

Hellenistic and Roman artists were apparently the first in the world to invent a manner of painting which could suggest light falling through the air, flowing between bodies and hills, trees and houses. In much the same way, Bischoff's paintings push back walls and open vistas of pearly atmosphere, of cascading cold, clear light receding to distant mountain peaks. The owner of one Bischoff, the writer Mark Schorer, has said: "When I get up in the morning, or come home at night, and walk into the room where our big Bischoff hangs, I walk into day." Like his Roman antecedents, Bischoff has found that these gracious vistas are enhanced by accents of warm color—flowers and masses of foliage that seem to bloom just beneath the paint surface and are seen as a blur in the corner of one's eye. Bischoff's figures, on the other hand, are painted with almost architectural solidity. Here he joins painters like the Frenchman Corot, who was inspired by the power of the Italian sunlight to give a marblelike solidity to objects. Yet Bischoff's works are touched by a muted romanticism, on the same intimate scale as Bonnard's, yet more sentimental. It is this tender absorption with the inner life of his subjects which is Bischoff's own contribution to the antique style he employs. His figures look away from the canvas surface, shrouded in concentration on a flower or the far horizon or—narcissuslike —on a reflection in an opalescent stream (see "Two Figures with Vermilion Light" and "Girl Wading" in the portfolio following page 16). The pantomime itself seems meaningful, like a single frame from a film. Perhaps the subject of this pantomime is—in the sense which Park described earlier—a passage toward "being yourself."

It is Park who most rigorously banishes himself from his art and comes closest to re-creating an impersonal, neoclassic style. If Bischoff's figures are wrapped in sentiment, Park's are stripped bare of personal reflections and might be idealizations of the American Youth. Hard chested, with slim waist, flat abdomen, columnar legs, thick neck, and the flat, blank regard of adolescence ("Standing Couple" and "Four Men"), a figure by Park makes a commanding impression not unreminiscent of that most ideal of all young men, the archaic Greek *kouros*. Now and then Park poses a figure in the classic posture of art-school models, a pose which Cézanne drew in his search for architectonic form: one foot advanced, weight on the back foot, hands on hips. Behind this stereotyped stance looms the classical ideal itself, and Park frequently makes direct reference to sculptured reliefs of pre-classic and classic Greece, with figures set in clear, deliberately cut-off planes of space. Sometimes the reference is direct: a figure assumes the hip-shot position standardized by Polyclitus, with arms disposed in quiet balance holding a fragment of drapery. In other works, African

Long-time friends and neighbors, the Berkeley trio have drawn each other at various times. Left to right: Bischoff by Park in wash, Park by Diebenkorn in pencil, and Diebenkorn by Bischoff in ink.

sculpture replaces the *kouros* as his model. "I love the urgency of primitive art," Park says, "the need, the anonymity." In some of his most recent paintings, a crudity of color and line, bordering on the expressionistic, and a sketchy, dabbed-on calligraphy introduce scattered notes of tension that may mark a new phase in Park's development.

Anonymity versus expressionism, the classic versus the primitive: much of Park's labor is directed toward uniting these opposites into what he calls a single "look." Diebenkorn apparently is involved in a similar, synthesizing program, except that his polarities have more to do with technique than with ideas. For like many of his colleagues, Diebenkorn has rejected the Renaissance system of perspective and, in so doing, has found himself face to face with an old dilemma of the Campanian painter: the reconciliation of near and far. Then the problem was expounded on frescoed walls: one reads it, indirectly, in a baffling split in the perspective treatment of background and foreground. Since artists had not yet learned the laws of perspective, objects in the foreground were painted from one point of view, and the background—houses, archways, or hills—from another. In Diebenkorn's new paintings, this same intriguing break in continuity between foreground and background, between the figure and the world, is expressed in a kind of double-jointed perspective like that on some Pompeian walls. Because of his uncanny gift for suggesting distant, light-saturated space, the dislocation between foreground and background in his pictures becomes even more apparent.

Diebenkorn's reluctance, or inability, to commit himself to the Renaissance system of perspective or some other more up-to-date principle of unification seems to be at the crux of his artistic and intellectual life. His compositions are the most ambitious and searching and, by the same token, the least realized of the Berkeley trio. His canvases could well be taken as comments on the difficulties of communication between the subject (with all its private associations for the artist) and the world. They seem to say that if these opposing forces cannot be joined together in the battle of the studio, then the subject must give way; for in a few recent works the figure has evaporated, leaving behind it, on the front plane of the composition, some spectral souvenir like a cup on a window sill or a chair half-turned ("Ocean View from Window"). Such a work may impress one with the same air of desolate incompleteness as a column left standing alone in an Italian field. Clear-spoken in spite of himself, Diebenkorn, when asked what kind of art he would like best to collect, answered: "The city of Pompeii."

Ever since the Renaissance, Rome and—after it was excavated—Pompeii have been a lodestone for painters absorbed in loving studies of the human body and open radiant landscape. There Corot painted his stony Italian scenes, which seem to be constructed out of light; however, since his time vanguard artists have gone there less and less often, preferring the grayer but more intellectually alive northern cities of Paris, London, and now New York, where they have created the studio-bound art of our time. Now these three California artists and a small group around them seem to be, perhaps unconsciously, repeating the classical Italian cycle. Yet having turned away from one kind of antinatural art, they hesitate on the brink of nature itself.

Using the figure as a subject, they still work without models in their studios. Bischoff is the only one of the three who regularly draws from the model; and his painting of the figure—though eventually done without reference to those drawings—is a far less labored act than the figure painting of his colleagues. Diebenkorn may make his first sketches from a model, but then, like Matisse, he reduces the figure through many distillations to its final, more or less abstracted state ("Coffee"). Park is the most outspoken against life drawing, even as practice for his hand or eye. Is this why his figures repeat themselves with a compulsive sameness, as though they were casts shelled-off from a figure once seen and then immured in his memory? As Kenneth Clark says in his book *The Nude,* "A contempt for drawing from life has great drawbacks." Clark is speaking here of Hogarth, the contemporary of the Italian-bent Constable and Turner. Like Park, Hogarth stayed in his studio and "disapproved of academic drawing from life and advocated the use of memory." Hence, "there is none of that absorption, that detached but loving contemplation, which makes a low subject great. So that . . . he remains a provincial master."

One senses a desire on the part of these three Berkeley artists to indulge in this kind of absorbed contemplation, but apparently they are stopped halfway by the modern taboo against imitating nature. The alternative has faced artists before. After the brilliant start which Roman painting made in Campania, it split into two styles. One left off probing the world and, under the influence of the Syrian Near East, became an art of abstract patterns based on those stiff, dark-eyed figures we call Byzantine. Diebenkorn's figures, after many transmutations, now move in this direction too, particularly toward the portraits of the Fayum, which he calls his favorite works of art. The other, or naturalistic, Roman style found its way underground as the Empire collapsed, but flowered again in the Renaissance, when not only painters but poets, scientists, and politicians joined in mastering the world. It is because Bischoff, Park, and Diebenkorn seem, in varying degrees, divided between these two fundamental avenues of art that their work today seems so poignant, so serious, and yet still tentative.

Eleanor C. Munro, whose article on "Portraits in Our Time" appeared in the January, 1959, issue of HORIZON, *is an art historian, critic, and contributing editor of* Art News.

WAS SOCRATES GUILTY AS CHARGED?

CONTINUED FROM PAGE 104

lack of fixed ethical principles, and to their irreverence. The tragic irony is that he was executed for their "crime" because of a persistent confusion, which we can trace as far back as Aristophanes's *Clouds*, first produced on the stage in 423 B.C. Socrates is the central comic character in that play, and the picture of him is about as false as can be. The playwright's Socrates is a conglomerate of the scientist-philosopher like Anaxagoras, of the Sophists, and of pure comic invention. Of the real Socrates there is little other than his poverty, and even that is caricatured.

I have no idea how much Aristophanes knew, in a systematic way, about the teaching of Anaxagoras and Protagoras and Socrates. But whether he was expert or not, the line he took was that distinctions were irrelevant. The whole lot were corrupters of youth, and what did it matter if one corrupted with his astronomy and another with his ethics, or if one took pay and the other did not? There were several reasons why Socrates was the choice victim for the cruel burlesque of *Clouds*. He was the best known of the various intellectuals under attack. Most of the others were foreigners who came and went; whereas Socrates was a citizen, a native of Athens, who was always there, in the most public places. He was poor and ascetic, proud of his simple clothes and his bare feet. He was ugly, a serious point. Just imagine small boys gaping from a safe distance at Socrates, with his satyr-like face, talking and talking and talking. Small boys grew up to be members of Aristophanes's audiences, and to be jurors at the trial of Socrates. Aristophanes was surely playing on currently popular themes. Although he did not invent them, he intensified them, and he must bear a heavy responsibility, at a distance, for the eventual trial and execution of Socrates.

The distance from *Clouds*, however, was twenty-four years. The question still remains: Why was Socrates put on trial in 399? By some chance, precisely as Plato said. Anytus and Meletus and Lycon joined together for personal reasons, which we can only guess at. That they were able to do so is no problem: personal grievances have been the root cause of many trials, in Athens as elsewhere. That they *succeeded*, however, can be explained only by the long complicated background I have been describing.

And yet, had only thirty-one jurors voted the other way, Socrates would have been acquitted in spite of everything, so close was the margin. There was no lynch psychology; there are even no indications that public emotions were wildly aroused. No one was creating a martyr. That came afterwards. To the people close to Socrates, and to others who were deeply interested in philosophy, this was no mere personal tragedy but something very much deeper and more universal in its meaning. It was these men who, in the next generation or two, created the symbol and the myth. The actual indictment, said Plato, was a matter of chance. But what lay behind it was not; it was inherent in any society in which power lay in the hands of any group simply because it had wealth or numbers or some other purely external qualification. Only the virtuous—the philosophers—should govern; otherwise there could be only evil consequences. Democracy was the worst form of misrule, but for Plato the death of Socrates symbolized the evil of any open or free society not just of a democratic one.

It was the nineteenth century, in particular, which abstracted one part from the myth created by Plato and seized on that side of it only, the dangers of mass rule. In truth, the fate of Socrates is a demonstration of the old axiom that eternal vigilance is the price of liberty. Freedom never sits so securely that it may not be harmed by its own upholders. In fifth-century Athens the elements of insecurity were both numerous and strong. There was the chronic poverty of resources, with its never-ending threat of famine; there was the long-drawn-out war with Sparta; there was the fact that freedom and democracy were, by definition, the privilege of a minority and excluded slaves and numerous noncitizens; and there was widespread superstition and irrationalism. There was also a technical weakness in the system. The juries had too much latitude, in the sense that they could not only decide on a man's guilt, but they could also define the crime he had committed. When impiety—and this is only an example—is a catch basin, no man is safe.

That much can be conceded to the myth in its modern version, but no more. The execution of Socrates is a fact, and it is one of several such facts which reveal that Athenian democracy was not a perfect instrument. It is equally a fact, which both ancient and modern spokesmen for the myth conveniently overlook, that the case of Socrates was isolated in its time. There could be no better witness to this than Plato. It was in Athens that he worked and taught, freely and safely, for most of his long life; and what he taught was hostile, down to its very roots, to much that Athenians believed and cherished. No one threatened him or stopped him. The Athenians are entitled to have their record judged whole for the two centuries in which they lived under a democracy, and not solely by their mistakes. So judged, it is an admirable record, an argument *for* a free society. Ironically both Plato and Xenophon (and some modern historians) idealized Sparta as against Athens. Sparta was the Greek closed society par excellence. There Socrates could never have *begun* to teach, or even to think.

M. I. Finley is an American classicist who lectures at Jesus College, Cambridge. An earlier article of his, "Thucydides' War," appeared in the January, 1960, issue of HORIZON.

THE TROJAN HORSELESS CARRIAGE

(A fragment from the entry, "USSR, History of," from the Great Soviet Encyclopaedia, Revised, 1970)

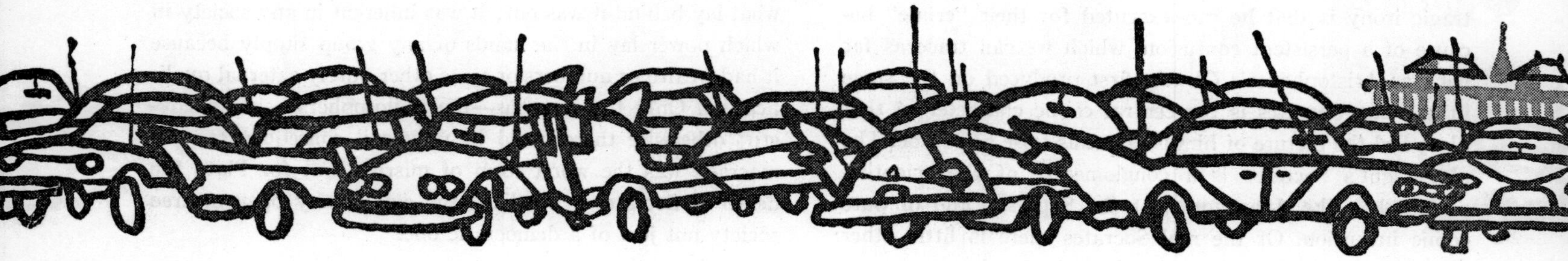

. . . Soviet progress had never reached greater heights, nor had the Marxist-Leninist peace offensive scored greater successes, than in the very year when, as we have now learned, the plotters of the imperialist camp managed to introduce their Trojan horse into the glorious motherland. It was in 1963 that the American government unexpectedly offered as a "gift" to the USSR one entire year's output of its automobiles. The Presidium of the Supreme Soviet, after a hurried meeting called by Party Chairman A. Mikoyan, at once announced that the offer was a trick, and several comrades pointed out that since capitalism never "gives" away anything, the automobiles unquestionably were intended to exploit the toiling Soviet masses. It was likely, suggested one member of the Central Committee, that beneath the imperialist professions of goodwill and generosity, one or more dark motives could be found. He felt sure that they were weapons of colonialist propaganda and perhaps instruments of germ warfare as well.

Just before an indignant refusal was sent to the Americans, however, Party Chairman Mikoyan took the floor to point out the dialectical errors in these views. The offer of all these cars was, he said, only orthodox capitalist behavior. The capitalist system was feeling the strain of the great Soviet industrial achievements, a condition widely noticed since the launching of Lunik, Marsnik, and Andromedanik. Forced to continue their mad pace of production, unable to withstand another depression without a revolution, desperate for markets, the Americans actually preferred to make their automobiles and give them away than to face the possibility of closing down their plants. He called the Committee's attention to the sacred writings of Marx, Engels, and Lenin on this very point. This was the crisis of capitalism at last. They must produce or perish, export or die.

"Comrades," he said, "this is a time for celebration. We might as well accept the automobiles!"

Thus the great mistake was committed. The government accepted the offer with Soviet graciousness: our ambassador in Washington presented the American president with a gold model of the new "Extermination for Peace" rocket, and there was a great reception for American representatives at the Kremlin. As a mark of official favor, very few of the Americans engaged in delivering the automobiles were arrested or interrogated for more than a week. But the reception by our workers and peasants was ecstatic. As the wretched American machines poured across the borders and unloaded at every port, the crowds became uncontrollable. Flowers were thrown. The people's police were unable to prevent the populace from leaping into the cars and driving away with them in all directions. Absenteeism at all farms and factories rose dramatically.

Aghast at this un-Soviet behavior, the Party discovered, too late, the extent of the propaganda defeat. Because of a criminal lack of preparation by the press, the people failed to recognize the uncultured nature of the capitalist automobiles or the need to turn them over at once to party authorities. Activists were sent out to nationalize the keys and take the cars away to state garages, but it turned out that there were no garages, owing to defective planning, and that the crafty Americans had furnished duplicate keys. As soon as the activists were out of sight, the undisciplined citizens leaped into the cars again.

It must be realized that there were six million U.S. cars, and that, in order to maintain face, it was necessary to accept a second year's shipment also, this time of eight million cars.

Now, it must be admitted, the Party compounded its error. Under a new One-Year Plan, all other production was cut back (even including the plans for Milky-Waynik) in order to outstrip capitalist production of automobiles. Comrade Mikoyan announced that Soviet production would be double that of the U.S.A. and that all Communist cars would be twice as long. At the end of only eleven months, the glorious motherland had, alas, exceeded these norms, producing 16,000,718 cultured Soviet passenger automobiles! The following year, in which the Americans shipped ten million cars, the Soviet Union produced twenty-five million. The space and arms programs were totally abandoned. Shock forces of people's volunteers from the other people's democracies in Eastern Europe, recruited to aid in production, had come in such numbers that large parts of Czechoslovakia, East Germany, Bulgaria, and Rumania were left with few inhabitants. Still the race went on, until, by early 1969, there were 203,000,000 automobiles of all kinds in the USSR, or one for every comrade.

Two hundred and three million automobiles! It is scarcely necessary, in these unhappy times, to remind the reader what effect all this had: not even the capitalist countries had ever seen such traffic, in rows as long as the notorious New York bread lines. In the cities the jams now lasted for five, ten, and fifteen hours. To reach a suburb or one's country *dacha* became an all-day expedition. The old airports, near the cities, were converted into parking areas but soon overflowed helplessly. The jet airports, many miles farther away, were almost totally inaccessible because of traffic. People who were traveling by air often did not come home for weeks or months, and a class of citizens grew up who simply lived at airports.

But what, comrades will ask, was taking place in the imperialist camp? What was happening in America, shipping all its automobile production to us? Relatively little

is known, owing to the destruction of records by the anti-Party group who, under Mikoyan, paid little heed either to our own agents or to the capitalist press, secure as they were in their misinterpretation of Lenin, sure as they were that the fascists were merely exporting their depression.

It is not known, for example, who conceived the capitalist plot, or its exact details. We do know, however, that the shipping out of the automobiles achieved a great change in the life of the U.S.A. As their older automobiles wore out, traffic thinned, on American highways, moving faster and faster. The cars that remained were able to be driven about rapidly in cities and to be parked almost anywhere their owners wished. For lack of automobiles, many citizens returned to riding in railways, which had formerly been at the point of extinction. Laden again with freight and passengers, they improved and multiplied their services. It became much safer to drive since the less careful motorists soon wrecked their cars and were usually unable to replace them. As trucks and buses left the highways, loss of life decreased, as did insurance rates and the discomforts of automobiling. In fact, motoring tended to resume its former place as a bourgeois sport. People came to work and to their appointments on time. Production increased. The growth of walking promoted health. As the air became purer, free of monoxide and other oil fumes, the incidence of lung cancer fell off noticeably. In this connection, one of our agents in the Los Angeles motion-picture colony reported that the smog had lifted in that city and it was possible to see without artificial lights during the day—an almost forgotten luxury in the Moscow of 1968 and 1969.

Although the Mikoyan group in the Central Committee stubbornly refused to face them, other more sinister results could soon be observed. As the Americans spent less and less time hunched mindless and slack-jawed over the wheels of their automobiles, the arts of reading and even of study revived. The despised American educational system began to move forward as rapidly as the celebrated Soviet one now declined. And on a more practical ground, the Americans, with so many fewer cars, found it no longer necessary to build roads. In some places, indeed, where roads had been built to excess—with superhighways crossing thruways which in turn vaulted over parkways which bypassed ordinary roads—it was possible to sell off and dismantle some of the uglier new construction. Taxes were reduced considerably, and the capitalist economy enjoyed a regrettably strong new lease on life, a fact which did not go unnoticed among the neutralist countries.

As is well known, however, the errors of Mikoyan and his gang were not really unmasked by events until May Day of 1969. On that fateful day, after unprecedented deliveries of new cars and gasoline, every vehicle in all the Russias turned out for the holiday, an event which can never be forgotten. Except in a few country districts, every road was jammed solid, without an inch between bumpers, by ten o'clock in the morning. And still more cars came—off the farms, from driveways, from cellars—until, by noon, nothing was moving from Leningrad to the Crimea, from the Urals to Moscow. There was not even enough room, especially with the comrades' tempers so heated, to back up or remove cars from the road. Only a handful of the usual throng turned up on foot at Red Square; the tanks and mobile guns of the parade itself never left the suburbs, where the tanks are still rusting to this day. Only one commissar reached the platform in front of Lenin's tomb, and he got there by helicopter.

Since the Central Committee was hopelessly decentralized by the traffic jam, only local action could be taken to relieve it. Derricks were mobilized in several cities to lift the cars out of the way, but they could not get close enough and soon ran out of fuel. Plans were proposed in several districts to bring up trains wherever the tracks crossed roads in order to push a few cars out of the way by brute force and thus provide maneuvering space, but it turned out that all the engines had rusted out after three years or more of disuse. Everything was thus frozen in place, and the citizens got out of their automobiles to start their long walks home. Unaccustomed to exercise, weakened by inhaling vast amounts of monoxide gas, hungry and disgusted, many of them gave voice to antistate remarks. With the roads clogged beyond hope, nearly everything stopped dead in European Russia—transportation, distribution, production, even government itself.

As of this moment, the picture of events is still not entirely clear. The Central Committee and Presidium have reorganized behind the Urals. News reaches us infrequently from European Russia, and it is not known what the state of government is there, although there are rumors of the presence of ostensible American Red Cross parties and one confirmed account of a food shipment from Iowa, doubtless part of an invasion headed by the well-known food-monger H. Hoover.

It is cold in this road-free portion of Siberia where the Soviet government is holding out, and most inaccessible. But at least there are no automobiles. For the mistake of A. Mikoyan is now clear to all comrades. It was an oversimplification of Marxist-Leninist doctrine to say the capitalists must export or die. Rather, they must export their automobiles or die of strangulation; this is the correct interpretation. And what Marx really said was: The automobile is the opium of the people.

By OLIVER JENSEN

PRIVACY LOST

CONTINUED FROM PAGE 6

Aspirin is knocking at the door of the duodenum, Mr. Laxative is dutifully hurrying toward the colon, and Mr. Nasal Decongestant is flushing the eight sinuses.

In such an enlightened age, no wonder Arthur Godfrey's ravaged lung and President Eisenhower's intestinal functions were front-page news. (Three days after the President's heart attack in 1955, James C. Hagerty told a news conference: "He had a good bowel movement." And according to the verbatim transcript, as printed in the New York *Times*, Dr. Paul Dudley White immediately explained: "Now I put that in. . . . I said the country will be very pleased—the country is so bowel-minded anyway—to know that the President had a good movement this morning, and it is important.") No wonder Christian Herter's arthritis warranted a special press conference, that Senator Wayne Morse felt entitled to ask Clare Boothe Luce's doctor if she had ever had psychiatric care, and that reporters felt it their sacred duty to chronicle the last painful days of John Foster Dulles. Marguerite Higgins spun her post-mortem over three days and many columns of type, and Ruth Montgomery in the New York *Journal-American* covered the death from the unusual point of view of Dulles's dog: "An inconsolable little black poodle named 'Pepi' Dulles took one look at his master's mortal remains today, moaned softly and collapsed into a corner. His long vigil was over, but an aching void remained. The person he loved best in all the world was dead."

While assaults on privacy come from many sides, it is amazing how many are self-inflicted. Any number of celebrities now disgorge their blackest secrets in print, as if hoping to banish their private demons by serving them at a public feast. From three such confessions an industrious scribe named Gerold Frank has mined one of the richest veins of metal (not gold) in recent literary annals. Frank is the ghost who put to paper Lillian Roth's *I'll Cry Tomorrow*, the late Diana Barrymore's *Too Much, Too Soon*, and Sheilah Graham's *Beloved Infidel*, books which together have sold more than 6,000,000 copies and earned $750,000, including foreign editions and royalties from the movies that Hollywood avidly made from all three.

In their books, Miss Roth and Miss Barrymore told explicitly how an overdose of husbands and liquor reduced them to squalid depths. "I told him [Gerold Frank] things I wouldn't have told a priest," Miss Barrymore said, and Frank obviously had the same powers of exorcism over Miss Graham. In her book she confessed that her real name was Lily Sheil, which she loathed, and that her upbringing was far shabbier than the one she had invented to conceal it. "The whole of my childhood," she said, "has been something dark and secret to me, and the name I was born with is tied up with the years I have kept hidden so long."

Miss Graham could have kept those years hidden forever. They are her business, or at least they would have been so regarded in any era but this. As for Frank, he has been closeted with Zsa Zsa Gabor, who promised to tell all, and there is no reason to think that she won't. *McCall's* seems to have no doubts, for it paid $100,000 to obtain the magazine rights.

Meanwhile, various other men and women have been purging themselves, from various motives, without benefit of ghostly intercession. Sometimes a book springs from an author's sincere desire to help others by revealing an intimate personal story. Such was Lael Wertenbaker's *Death of a Man*, an account of her writer husband's losing fight against cancer and of the extraordinary compact she made with him as the fight neared its end. Rarely has such an excruciatingly private experience been set down in print. On the other hand, Norman Mailer's *Advertisements for Myself*, a running tale of his experiments with drink, drugs, and sex, can only be regarded as a psychiatric self-treatment carried on in public.

Disrobing in public has even taken literal form. The mother-in-law of the painter Larry Rivers once posed for him in the nude, and he exhibited the full-length portrait with the subject identified. During their marriage, Linda Christian and the late Tyrone Power not only had themselves painted nude to the waist, but hung the portraits in their house and invited *Look* to publish photographs of them in its pages.

Such exhibitionism is not uncommon among people of artistic bent. What *is* uncommon is for a country's dignitaries to drop their public mask and help a photographer perform a jocular stunt, as dozens do in Philippe Halsman's recent *Jump Book*. Halsman persuaded his renowned subjects—including Vice President Richard Nixon (see page 4), Adlai Stevenson, J. Robert Oppenheimer, Judge Learned Hand, and board chairman John J. McCloy of the Chase Manhattan Bank—to jump for him. "One of our deepest urges," he says, "is to find out what the other person is like," and with this portfolio of leaders who don't have their feet on the ground, he has gone a long way toward gratifying that urge. But could he have persuaded America's eminent men to take to the air twenty years ago?

Perhaps the snooping instinct has been sharpened by the kind of magazine reporting that delves as deeply into a man as gall and tenacity will permit. *Time* boasts that its researchers spend weeks with the subject of a "cover" story, detecting mannerisms that doubtless a wife or husband never noticed, and the *New Yorker* "Profiles" are born of an FBI-like search through the patient's past. These techniques have undoubtedly inspired legions of newspapermen. Sidney Skolsky is only being true to modern journalism's creed when he asks every Hollywood star if he (or she) sleeps in pajama tops, bottoms, or neither.

Serious writing has also suffered some strange inroads.

Before television, authors generally worked in seclusion while publishers tried to sell their books. Now it is necessary to sell the man also, and all publishers try hard to get their writers invited onto the programs of Paar, Garroway, and other TV hosts, who thus have become influential literary arbiters. Rare is the author, like J. D. Salinger, who refuses to undergo promotion acts and interviews of any kind.

To be sure, most writers are too shy to do themselves much good on a TV show. On the other hand, all sorts of entertainers have suddenly blossomed into "authors"—and best-selling authors, too. They go from show to show touting themselves, their own books, and one another's books; and this accounts for the success—unaccountable by literary standards—of such volumes as *My Brother Was an Only Child* and *Charley Weaver's Letters from Mamma,* written respectively by the gagman Jack Douglas and the professional hayseed Cliff Arquette, both chronic visitors to the Paar show.

The "public relations consultant" has become entrenched as one of the high priests of modern America. His sole purpose is to knead the public image of his client, like a lump of clay, into a fresh and attractive shape. In some cases this can mean a lot of kneading, for he is often called upon to repair a reputation that is damaged almost beyond salvage.

"Let's say there's a guy in New York who's the vice-president of a bank," says Benjamin Sonnenberg, probably the ablest clay modeler around. "He comes from a fine family. The family escutcheon was once a wondrous shining object, but now it has become slightly tarnished. Our client has gotten divorced a couple of times, he runs around with a fast crowd, his name appears in the tabloids. . . . What I do for him is simple: I breathe on the family escutcheon and he polishes while I breathe." Translated, this means that the playboy is turned into an exemplary citizen—or at least into the public image of one.

Yet such major overhauls, for which the PR industry was founded and on which it fed in its early years, are now only a small part of the consultant's job. Today his task is not so much to shine an image that has tarnished as to create one where none existed before. Hitherto faceless and diligent corporation presidents, bankers, and other executives by the hundreds have allowed themselves to be converted into "personalities" by such puppeteers as Sonnenberg, Edward L. Bernays, and the late Carl Byoir on the theory that a corporation is more lovable if its officers are, too. To sell the man is to help sell the product, and the fact that there are 1,200 public relations firms in the nation today (Manhattan listed ten in 1935) indicates that man-selling has become a brisk business. Its techniques are usually visible in the man who is being sold. It is not just that his dress, his house, his taste in sports or art or entertainment are made topics of public interest; his whole manner, including his homey references when he makes a speech or the very shape of his haircut, if by chance he is a presidential possibility, begins to look as if it were a product of a premeditated campaign.

Sonnenberg brought his most famous Galatea to life in the person of Charles Luckman, an aggressive young vice-president of the Pepsodent tooth paste company, who under PR coaching blossomed into a tweedy, pipe-smoking liberal business statesman and rapidly became president of Pepsodent and then of the greater Lever Brothers combine. Under Sonnenberg's coaching he was already moving into the higher echelons of government service when, back at the factory, he was caught asleep at the big switch from soap to detergents. The young president made a hasty exit, turning to the profession of architecture (where he has since done well). For one who created the Luckman legend, Sonnenberg took its collapse with remarkable equanimity. It wasn't *his* fault, Sonnenberg said, that Luckman failed to live up to his billing.

One of privacy's last preserves, in most countries, is "society." Society is founded, after all, on the principle of excluding the masses from the pleasures and preserves of the fortunate few. It is also founded on a basic canon of manners. "Not to attract attention to oneself in public is one of the fundamental rules of good breeding," says Emily Post. "Nothing stamps the vulgarian more plainly than advertising his possessions or achievements by loud word of mouth."

The old order of decorum that decreed that a lady's name should appear in the newspaper on only three occasions—her birth, her marriage, and her death—is now maintained only by a small and shrinking aristocracy, while the new society includes women who hire press agents at $100 to $150 a week to get their names in print as often as possible.

The new elite's ascent has been swift in the years since World War II, thanks to the boom in charity appeals, charity balls (as against old-fashioned private balls), and their privacy-invading cousin, the house-and-garden tour, all of which are administered by committees of moneyed ladies. Dowagers of the old society still head many of these committees and shun personal publicity, but they will add to their committee a lady of the new society who contributes generously to the cause. Then the two ladies appear together in a picture on the newspaper's society page, and Mrs. Arriviste has arrived.

Soon she is heading charity committees herself and shrewdly crossing the trail of publicists all over town. In New York she will dine at the Colony, confident that the Colony's press agent will confect a column item about her new dress. She will patronize a "society hairdresser" who has a press agent to report the visits of just such patronesses, and her designer, furrier, modiste, shoe salon, and jeweler will be similarly staffed. Their various press agents may, as a matter of fact, be the same man—and also the lady's personal press agent—for there are a small number of publicists, like Count Lanfranco Rasponi and Emmett Davis, who specialize in this field and have interlocking accounts.

Ladies of the new society also invite the press to their private social affairs. "I'm asked to many parties," says Eugenia Sheppard, fashion columnist of the New York *Herald Tribune*, "for no reason except that the hostesses expect me to write about them, and when I go I meet all the other fashion and society reporters." Certain ladies do indeed turn up with astonishing frequency in the New York papers. It doesn't take a puzzle expert, for instance, to locate Mrs. Winston ("Cee-Zee") Guest or Mrs. Thomas M. ("Peggy") Bancroft, Jr., in print roughly once a day.

Publicity seekers also seek publicity these days by endorsing a commercial product. This used to be beneath the dignity of citizens in ordinary channels of life—such things were left to athletes and actors. Now all manner of celebrities and near celebrities participate. Ernest Hemingway has endorsed Ballantine Ale, for instance, and Leonard Bernstein, the pleasures of Puerto Rico. The publisher-columnist Bennett Cerf is a multiple endorser, and society ladies frequently turn up in advertisements cooing over their favorite eye shadow or shampoo. So popular has this form of appearance in public become that a company called Endorsements, Inc., was launched after World War II to help advertising agencies find endorsers. Evidently it found plenty, for it grosses more than a million dollars a year.

This abdication of privacy "is now acceptable . . . for a fee or in some cases for the reciprocal publicity," says Emily Post's successor as public arbiter of taste, Amy Vanderbilt, in her *Complete Book of Etiquette*. But "the boundaries of good taste should never be overstepped. You could permit yourself [in the endorsement] to be called 'wealthy' or 'socially prominent,' but not 'the heiress to $20,000,000.' "

Ordinarily, to have a divorce announced in public is the penalty a celebrity pays for his fame. Private citizens are relieved that on this unhappy occasion they can go their separate ways in private. Yet one New York executive and his wife, on parting recently, felt they could not simply leave the matter there. They sent to their acquaintances a formal card, engraved after the manner of a wedding announcement, which declared to one and all that John and Mary Doe, "with mutual sadness, have chosen this way of letting our friends know of our divorce. Both of us would be grateful if you just sort of accepted our decision, didn't ask us a lot of questions, and kept on liking both of us . . . as we shall, always, continue to like each other."

So far have the barriers fallen that few of us think of invoking our legal and moral rights to privacy. As a people, we are endearingly nice to strangers who pester us at the door or on the phone, apologizing elaborately for not doing what they ask. We can seldom bring ourselves to ask the cabby to turn down the radio or to put out his pestilential cigar. Not to call a man "Jim" or "Bill" from the first handshake is to sully the notion that we are all old pals together in the great Waring Blendor called America.

We might well recall the classic discussion of the legal right to privacy by the late Louis D. Brandeis and Samuel D. Warren in the *Harvard Law Review* of 1890:

"The intensity and complexity of life, attendant upon advancing civilization, have rendered necessary some retreat from the world. . . . Solitude and privacy have become more essential to the individual; but modern invention and enterprise have, through invasions upon his privacy, subjected him to mental pain and distress far greater than could be inflicted by mere bodily injury."

Yet even today, only rarely does a knight rise in full view to hurl back the intrusive enemy, and when he does so, it is an exhilarating moment. One such moment was Randolph Churchill's reply to John Wingate, when that TV interviewer asked a nosy question on his "Night Beat" program (March 6, 1958) about "the arrest of your sister Sarah in California." Churchill snapped: "I do not intend to discuss it with you. I never discuss matters relating to my family with total strangers. I wouldn't think of asking you about your sisters. Why the hell should I let myself be bullied around and kicked around by you? Your shame is on your own head."

Equally brisk and eloquent was young Steven Rockefeller's answer last year to reporters angry at being barred from his church wedding in a small town in Norway. "You represent the freedom of the press and I represent the privacy of an individual," he said. "To me this church service is a religious occasion and I am not a public figure."

What other oases of privacy remain? They can be counted almost on the fingers of a first baseman's mitt. One, paradoxically, is the commuter train. Though it is densely packed with men on its morning and evening journey, the man in the next seat occupies an inviolate island of silence, even if he is a close friend. Another oasis is the gentlemen's club. In that temple, Emily Post brooks nothing but spartan self-control. "It is one of the unbreakable rules not to speak to anybody who is reading or writing," she says, and she might have added sleeping. "If a new member happens to find at the club no one whom he knows, he goes about his own affairs. He either reads, writes, or looks out the window, or plays solitaire, or occupies himself as he would if he were alone in a hotel."

Sometimes, in the strangling streets of Manhattan, a relic of privacy's golden age comes purring by and gives the heart a momentary lift. It is a shiny cabriolet, its rear seat windowless and almost hidden from view. But in those dark shadows a bright object occasionally glitters. Is it the diamond choker of a very old lady going to tea with a girlhood friend? Is it the stickpin of a very old tycoon bound for his bank vault? Nobody on the sidewalk knows, and nobody will.

William K. Zinsser's unflinching eye served him well as movie critic of the New York Herald Tribune. *Now, as a free-lance writer, he is turning it on other aspects of the contemporary scene that seem tc him equally worthy of sardonic comment.*

EERO SAARINEN

CONTINUED FROM PAGE 82

better than what they replaced. We have better space, better apartments, more light, but we have destroyed the street façade. Now the street façade at its best is a very beautiful thing. Paris is made out of the street façades of buildings. We have destroyed that kind of concept, and instead we are building independent blocks. These are terribly torn things, and in many cases the architecture is very bad.

INTERVIEWER: How can the architect assume more responsibility for urban unity?

SAARINEN: I think the Yale colleges are an example of that kind of responsibility. We not only designed the buildings for the site, but we also considered the university's master plan, which goes beyond the present stage into the next, and made recommendations for that as well as for the master plan of the city of New Haven. I'm sort of proud of that kind of responsibility.

INTERVIEWER: Responsibility that goes beyond pure architecture?

SAARINEN: Responsibility beyond what has usually been associated with architecture as a profession. The architect's role is expanding in every direction. In the case of the Dulles International Airport in Washington, the first commercial airport designed exclusively for jets—which in some ways is the most exciting job we have done—no one asked us to grapple with the problem of a jet-age terminal beyond questions of pure architecture. But together with the engineers, Amman and Whitney, and Burns and McDonnell, and the economic consultant, Charley Landrum, and all of the others—really, a very large team—we created an entirely new system of passenger handling and had to deal with the consequences of all that. The first consideration, before we even thought of the design of the building, was to find some way of shortening the enormous distances which passengers now walk to planes, through the terminals and the "fingers" that extend from them. Take an airport with sixty gates, and assume 200 feet for each gate position; if you string them in a row, the airport itself would be 12,000 feet long. So we decided to investigate the problem and started a whole research program in our own office. We wanted to find out exactly what happened at airports in order to avoid building still another unsatisfactory terminal. In fact, we bought stop watches and counters, and sent men out to Willow Run, to Dallas, to Chicago, to Washington, and to many other places just to find out certain facts. And gradually the concept of a mobile lounge—a part of the terminal which detaches itself from the building and travels out to the plane—seemed more and more feasible.

INTERVIEWER: On the order of the bus system used at some European airports?

SAARINEN: Yes, but not quite. I remember somebody once said that the American public will never accept a step-down in convenience for another step-up in technology. To add a bus to the process of getting from the ticket counter to the plane is a negative thing. I've been particularly angry in London, where they have buses with two-foot-wide doors. I always carry as much as possible so that I'm not over the weight—cameras and night bags and coats—and I can't get through those doors. Now, instead of a bus, how can one make something that is luxurious? Then it struck us: by combining the departure lounge and the moving vehicle into a single convenience, and by combining *that* with a covered gangplank which hitches directly to the plane.

INTERVIEWER: What was the next step in the design procedure?

SAARINEN: You have to remember that these steps are just like shingles. They overlap, and many things go on at the same time. We all worked on the ramp, on the area where the planes are parked, and finally, in a joint meeting, we adopted a scheme by Burns and McDonnell for what is really a giant gas station. The planes taxi into the station, where they refuel and receive the passengers, and then they go straight to the take-off position. It sounds simple, but it took a lot of planning.

INTERVIEWER: And you started on the terminal building itself only after these problems were resolved?

SAARINEN: We started thinking of the building as soon as the mobile-lounge concept seemed feasible, and actually it came rather simply once the difficult planning and programing were worked out. The site was basically very simple. There were no other buildings around, and the only problem was that of approaching a building on a flat plain. In a way, architecture is really placing something between earth and sky. And then there was the spirit of the building, the gateway to Washington. The tradition of Federal architecture is static, but an airport should be essentially nonstatic; and we thought that if these traditions could be brought together, we would have a very interesting building. We came to the conclusion that a strong form hovering over the plain would look best.

INTERVIEWER: And the great suspended roof developed from that?

SAARINEN: At first we did not see it as a hanging roof at all, but more like the curved roof that Corbu put on Ronchamp. Then we saw the roof as high in front, low in the middle, and a little higher in back, to shelter the incoming passengers, and it occurred to us that this could be done as a suspended structure. Then we discussed it with Amman and Whitney to find out if it would be feasible structurally and economically, and they got rather enthusiastic. So the form came first and the structural justification later. Now this is O.K. if the justification comes, but if it doesn't, it really gets to look awful; it's phony.

INTERVIEWER: How do you rank Dulles International among your buildings? Would you single out any special significance for it as a work of art?

SAARINEN: Its significance, I would say, is that I think it will be a hell of a good airport. In relation to my own career, I think it is a continuation of exploring the problem of concrete and exploring the problems of Federal character—it is an entrance to the capital, after all—and airport character. I don't know how it ranks with our other buildings because it isn't finished yet and there are still many, many problems to be solved. I think of it as a completely logical, imaginative, and responsible answer to the problem. In other words, I feel that we shouldn't look at it only as a work of art. We should look at it as an architect's problem in total relation to the present world, and I hope as such we have done a good job.

Allan Temko, who frequently writes about art and architecture for HORIZON, *is an associate editor of* Architectural Forum.

THE COMING FLOOD OF PHARAOH'S TEMPLES

CONTINUED FROM PAGE 14

and emblem of the goddess Hathor, to whom the temple was dedicated. The wall decoration consists entirely of scenes representing offerings to various deities by the king and the queen. The second chamber is a small sanctuary in which a full-face image of the cow-goddess Hathor emerges from the rock. Standing before her is her son and heir, Ramses II, who shares in the homage that he and his consort, Nefertari, pay to the goddess everywhere on the temple walls.

Ramses II created Abu Simbel to implant respect for Egypt, her religion, and her culture among peoples always eager to intrigue against her. There he commemorated important events of his reign, recording them always in a manner that heightened the impression of Egyptian power. For example, when the Pharaoh married the daughter of the king of the Hittites in 1264 B.C., he ordered a stele carved alongside the terrace of the great temple. Fragments of copies of this "Marriage Stele," which provides one of the longest and most valuable historical texts in Egypt, have been found at Karnak, Aswan, and even Amara, in the Sudan, showing how widely Ramses circulated his version of the occasion. In it there is no indication that the marriage was, in fact, intended to strengthen an alliance concluded between the Hittites and the Egyptians thirteen years earlier or that the two nations were equals. Instead, Ramses shows the Hittites humbly submitting to Egyptian overlordship.

The upper part of the stele represents Ramses II seated under a baldachin between Ptah and Seth, the great god of the Hittites. To the right, the Hittite princess, already wearing the crown of the Egyptian kingdom, comes forward, followed by her father, who wears a high conical hat and raises his arms in a gesture of adoration. The Hittite king's declaration to Ramses, intended to set the tone for the sentiments of vassals toward Egypt, is inscribed in columns above him:

I adore thy beauty. . . . Thou art the child of Seth in truth. He has assigned the land of Kheta [*the country of the Hittites*] *to thee. I have despoiled myself of all my possessions, my eldest daughter at the head of them, to offer them to thy goodly countenance. Thou commandest us all. I am under thy feet eternally and forever, as well as all the land of Kheta. Thou hast appeared on the throne of Re* [*the Sun-god*]. *Every land is under thy feet forever.*

Under this scene, the first twenty lines are devoted to a hyperbolic eulogy of Ramses. Then comes history, written from the Egyptian point of view. The indecisive battle of Kadesh is transformed into a brilliant victory for Ramses, after which the Egyptian king is said to have stubbornly refused to accept tributes from the Hittites—although, in actual fact, the Hittites had not the slightest intention of offering him any.

The text of the marriage proclamation does not appear in its entirety on the Marriage Stele. There was not room. It was, however, enough to instruct and enlighten the Nubian tribes: the example of submission by the powerful king of the Hittites and the resulting benefit to his people.

The rest of the story has been reconstructed from the fragments of other versions of the inscription found at Aswan and at Karnak. On her arrival at the royal palace—doubtless at Tanis—the Hittite king's daughter greatly pleased Ramses, who found her beautiful. So he elevated her to the rank of queen and gave her an Egyptian name, Mat-neferu-Re—She Who Sees the Beauty of the Sun—which, in the inscription, is encircled by a cartouche, as was fitting for the official wife of a Pharaoh.

The Marriage Stele is not the only significant historical document preserved at Abu Simbel. Visitors are always shown an inscription in archaic Greek, engraved among many others—Greek, Carian, and Phoenician—on the leg of the headless colossus to the left of the main entrance. It was carved by Greek mercenaries who served under the redoubtable Pharaoh, Psamtik II, and dates from about 660 B.C.

King Psamtik having come to Elephantine, those who were with Psamtik, son of Theocles, beyond Kerkis as far as the river permitted, have written this: Potasimto led the foreigners and Amasis the Egyptians. We have written this, Arkhon, son of Amoibikhos, and Pelekos, son of Oudamos.

This inscription was long ago correlated with the information supplied by Herodotus concerning a revolt of Egyptian troops stationed at Elephantine. Disgusted at not having been relieved for three years, they deserted to the Ethiopians: "Psamtik, having been informed, pursued them. When he had overtaken them, he attempted by many words to dissuade them from forsaking their national gods, as well as their children and their wives. It is said that one of them, exhibiting his private parts, replied that wherever they might be, there would be children and wives. The troops, when they had continued to Ethiopia, gave themselves over to the king of the Ethiopians and were well rewarded."

The incident is full of life and the retort salty. It seems that the passage of Egyptian troops, reinforced by Greek mercenaries—to which the graffiti on the colossus at Abu Simbel testify—occurred during the course of the pursuit, before Psamtik overtook the fugitives and was treated to the tart rebuff.

In the temples at Abu Simbel the propaganda employed by Ramses II is obvious. The immensity of the statues, the battle scenes, the fettered Asiatic and Nubian prisoners depicted in notable reliefs on the foundations, the same captives shown being dragged before the gods as offerings—everything is done to inculcate the idea of the Egyptian king's superhuman power and the madness of opposing him. But

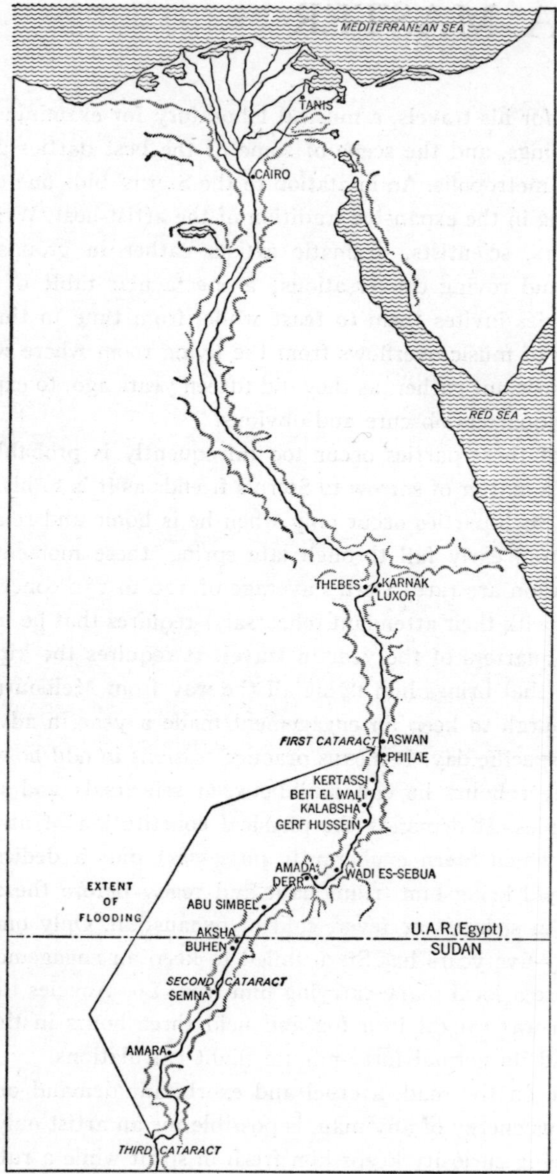

The new dam at Aswan will create a lake stretching along the Nile Valley for 300 miles. Facing inundation are scores of ancient monuments; sites of the most notable appear above.

the message rendered so clearly in the architecture and decoration of the buildings is even more explicitly expressed by the words of the temple inscriptions, and especially on the stele that is wedged between the last colossus to the north and the rock wall of the small temple.

This stele, which Barsanti cleared of sand in 1910, contains thirty-six lines of hieroglyphs. The first twenty-four are devoted to praises of Ramses II, after which comes a warning:

The King of Upper and Lower Egypt, User-maat-
Re Setep-en-Re, Son of Re, Meriamon Ramses,
he says:
Hearken to what I tell you, all ye people, princes
who are upon earth and warriors all!
I am Re, lord of heaven, on earth,
Who does things of benefit to you accordingly as
you work for him.
I am an effective protection for him who obeys him.
I do not sail with the wind of those who abandon
my affairs;
I sail the waters of my father.
I tread his road.
I came forth from the womb equipped in valor and
strength, ready, mighty and renowned in battle,
Coming as a child of god,
And established upon his throne.
They who behold me prosper;
They rejoice in me as in Horus, son of Isis, the
beloved;
They boast in pronouncing my name, as that of the
Lord of Nefret.
Confident is my stride; I traverse the lands with
speed, reaching the end of the winds.
The chiefs of the foreign lands come to me—those
who are ignorant of Egypt, those who have been
in revolt since the time of the god.
The princes approach me crying "Shalom!"
They cry before me, saying "At thy service! At thy
service!"
Like dogs fearing a stick
Their hearts choke because of me,
Quakings are in their bodies.
My dignity has confronted them, pervading their
limbs;
My name, it has made them tremble like that of
the lord of Ombos
When he hurls himself on the miserable Hittites to
their woe.
Their encampments are cast to the ground,
Their settlements have turned into flames,
Because he razes the land of Kheta,
As has come to pass since I proved myself chieftain.
Upper and Lower Egypt, User-maat-Re Setep-
en-Re, son of Re, of his body, whom he loves,
master of the crowns, Ramses Meriamon, en-
dowed with life like Re, eternally and forever.

Considered in itself, this message addressed by Ramses II to all peoples and all ages may seem grandiloquent. But if we read it against the background of the misfortunes that Egypt had undergone even from the period of the Pyramids—the social upheavals that had ruined her, the incessant foreign invasions that had so sorely tried her—and the disappointments that the future held in store for her at the hands of the Assyrians and the Persians, we must admit that it has a note of pathos that is not without greatness.

THE MAKING OF A MASTER

CONTINUED FROM PAGE 75

free until midnight, to be replaced yet by others coming off the radio networks who wanted to play from midnight until dawn. Scientists and musicians would wander in at any hour, sprawling on couches, sitting on the floor, squatting under the piano—all talking, then all rapt, all verbally or instrumentally exploring the meaning of sound and music. It was, as Stern recalls it, a total immersion in music, a total examination technically, intellectually, emotionally of music, a steeping of fiber and gland in the excitement of war, science, and music at once—from which he emerged with a range of control, confidence, and understanding that was the beginning of a freedom to grow as he wished.

Out of this period of a year and a half came Stern's first great impact on the critics of New York: his famous Carnegie Hall recital of January, 1943, a recital hailed by Virgil Thomson, the acerb critic of the *Herald Tribune*, as marking Stern's emergence as "one of the world's master fiddle players."

From 1943 on, Stern's career reads, like so many great triumphs, almost as an extravagant cliché—first recognition, then fame, then global acceptance. By 1945 Stern had reached a pace of ninety concerts a year in America. By 1948 he was ready for his first European performances, and the first acclaim there of an American-trained artist as a major figure of music in his own right. In Paris, Brussels, London, Rome, from the Salle Gaveau to the Vienna Konzerthaus, the tones of Stern announced that in America a new culture had produced its first master violinist. He participated in each of the three great Casals Festivals in southern France in the early fifties to help make that episode a watershed in musical history. By 1956, as the Cold War thawed, it was natural that the Russians should choose Stern as the first American invited to play on the Moscow concert stage in more than a decade.

Today Stern's international audiences draw him around the world in ever wider swings, and his average of 120 to 150 concerts a year carries him an approximate 100,000 miles annually. He has played on every continent and in almost every country where people gather to hear music—except Germany. As for Germany, where he refuses to play, Stern shares the emotions of his wife, whom he met on a concert tour of Israel when she had only freshly recovered from years of Nazi imprisonment.

Now, at forty, a sturdy, round-faced, powerfully built man of quenchless enthusiasm and Balzacian gusto, Stern carries his fame as lightly as he takes his music seriously. An anecdotalist of enormous range in four languages and half a dozen variants of the American, a trencherman and a gourmet of equal capacity and discrimination, he lives now in a duplex penthouse on the apartment cliffs overlooking Central Park, which is at once home for his two children, a base camp for his travels, a musical laboratory for examining his recordings, and the scene of some of the best parties given in the metropolis. An invitation to the Sterns' bids one to an evening in the expansive tradition of the artist-host. Writers, painters, scientists, dramatic artists gather in groups for wild and roving conversations; a spectacular table of cold delicacies invites them to feast while, from time to time, a billow of music overflows from the living room where working musicians gather, as they did fifteen years ago, to explore string quartets obscure and obvious.

That these parties occur too infrequently is probably as much a matter of sorrow to Stern's friends as it is to his wife Vera. Such parties occur only when he is home and relaxed, and from early fall through late spring, these moments of relaxation are rare. Stern's average of 120 to 150 concerts a year (with their attendant rehearsals) requires that he invest three-quarters of the year in travel. It requires the kind of travel that brings him flying all the way from Melbourne to Edinburgh to keep an engagement made a year in advance for a specific day. It means practice sessions in odd hotels at whatever hours he can find between rehearsals and plane schedules. It demands the physical constitution of an athlete (which Stern exuberantly possesses) plus a dedication that will bring him triumphant and ready before the audience, in sickness or fever, cold or exhaustion. Only once in twenty-five years has Stern failed to keep an engagement—because a local plane carrying him from Los Angeles to San Diego was caught in a fog and held three hours in the air beyond its normal forty-minute flight calculations.

Life on the road, a cruel and exorbitant demand on the nervous energy of any man, is possible for an artist only if a vitalizing curiosity keeps him fresh in spirit while a ruthless discipline governs that curiosity. Stern possesses both the curiosity and the discipline in necessary measure. He can return revived and bubbling with new information from a long train conversation with a group of electronics engineers on the mysteries of computers; or he can sleep, almost at will, sitting up or lying down in plane seat or Pullman when he feels it necessary. Normally, Stern tries to arrive at the scene of his next engagement the night before a scheduled concert or rehearsal so that he may wake the next morning in the city where he must play. He will have a late lunch before a concert—usually between three and four—and then not eat again until he has performed, passing the afternoon with a cat nap, a further rehearsal, occasionally a baseball or football game, or a movie (he is an *aficionado* of Westerns and thrillers). Gregarious, Stern frequently follows a concert with a late party organized for him by friends acquired over years in the cities he has visited. Such receptions run from the glitter of a Rothschild drawing room on Paris's Avenue Foch, through the pomp of an American embassy in Moscow or New Delhi, to the simplicity of middle-western American homes where he has been visiting for twenty years.

The drafts such a life makes on strength and nerves are replenished each summer by vacation, spent sometimes in Europe, sometimes in New England, with his wife and family. It is a period for committing new pieces to memory and repertoire, for reading new scores (last year, Stern read some forty scores of new violin compositions seeking those which could be given their first public hearing by his bow), and for restoring the muscular and neural controls which a year of total abrasion in travel and music wears thin. It is a time of listening again to his own music, of weighing the music he makes himself, contemplating, as he puts it, "how close to the truth" he is getting. For in Stern's eyes he is still unfinished, still reaching, still straining for that irretrievable beauty which music always promises and which, however close an artist comes to it, he can never totally possess.

It is difficult and perhaps impossible to define Stern's position in the world of music today beyond the round phrase of one commentator that Stern is both "the youngest of the great musicians and the greatest of the young musicians." Yet many people try.

There are some who regard Stern as a particularly American phenomenon, a brilliant mixture of all those various influences that have swept the American concert hall to create in the New World a new art. These are people who, explaining the matchless performance of American orchestras, reconstruct its origins from the migration here of Russian string players, German brass players, French woodwind players, and Italian conductors, all of whom could meet only in America to merge their special excellences. Out of their interacting influence has come that sheen, that splendor of sparkle without any apparent orchestral gaps, which is now the special American mark of symphonic performance. Such influence tracers, as they study Stern's playing, hear in him a flowing-together of all the tributaries of American music. Out of the polyglot musical chatter and phrasing in English-French-Russian-Italian-German-Yiddish that babbles backstage in every great American symphony orchestra, Stern has found a voice of his own, a combination of them all.

Others see Stern in a broader frame, in that stream of musical philosophy culminating in the influence of the superb Pablo Casals, which holds that music must be clear, must be expressive, must speak ideas, and that all techniques must be subordinated in the one golden clarity of communication. For such people, music is only an expression of the total culture of a time and people refracted through the experience of one man; and in Stern's playing, they hear the buried resonance of all he has taken from American life, from the physics of destruction to the beauty of the high arc of a baseball streaking down from the sky.

Stern himself, now graver and more withdrawn than formerly, occasionally sees himself with a flash of his earlier romantic exuberance as a bridge character—a man somehow fortunate enough to have absorbed the experiences of all the older schools and the arts of Koussevitzky, Toscanini, Casals, yet speaking for and responsible to a younger generation of American musicians for whom he must synthesize the eternities of past generations with the spirit of the present.

It is thus probably futile to try to separate out the great influences that have come together in Stern's art. "What you learn," said Alexander Schneider, a great violinist in his own right, speaking of his friend Isaac Stern lately, "is after you stop learning. And the thing about Isaac is that he is always learning, he has learned from all. He is the most alert, the most sensitive, the most responsive concert artist in America today. This amazing alertness to everything around him is always in his music. Most musicians are afraid to take from others because they are afraid of giving up their own identity. But Isaac is strong enough to take from everyone without losing his identity."

To grasp that identity, one must listen to Stern playing, say, the Mozart G major Concerto, and hear again the exquisite melancholy of the young Mozart in the adagio, the entire orchestra tiptoeing after Stern's violin, the orchestra muted yet pulsing to the violin's liquid rhythm—then hear the pause between movements as violin and orchestra break into the prancing, dancing rondo. Or, one must hear the violin assume the powerfully masculine quality of Bach's A minor Concerto, its architecture now made so inexorably clear by the stroke of the bow that it seems like a marble temple, and then, by a quiver of aural magic, becoming soft and transparent and a vision of something that never was.

Sometimes, in an appealing baritone, privately to a friend or in rehearsal, Stern will sing the phrases of the music he is about to perform, explaining what the fiddle is about to say. At other times he will hum and press his fingers on the knee of an interlocutor in variations of one passage, drumming softly with his fingertips to underscore the alternate moods he can draw from a single passage by the tiniest changes of timing or rhythm. But even after he has explained it, it becomes clear only after he has marched onto the stage and said it out with bow and string.

The artist's pause before performance—the halt of the dramatic star as he thrusts out his first line when the curtain goes up, the stillness of the musician before the baton falls—has always intrigued me. I asked Stern not long ago what it is he thinks of in that moment of pause before performance. "In the back of my head," he said, "I'm listening. It's singing to me. My inner ear says there is the dry sound, there is the warm sound, there is the white sound. It's speaking to me. Sometimes I can even hear the whole thing at once."

A love of music has accompanied Theodore H. White over his years as foreign correspondent, political reporter, and story teller (his new novel is The View from the Fortieth Floor*).*

THE MOMENT OF TRUTH

A literary red flag by Stephen White...

Christians and other barbarians, when introduced into a pride of ravenous lions on the floor of an arena, were generally good for a laugh or two, but it is a matter of record that the Romans required novelty in their divertissements. Someone conceived the ingenious idea of tossing foreigners to an angry bull, and thus a noble sport was born.

The scheme, at the outset, called for the bull to win, for the Romans were a kindly people and liked to see the fauna survive. Unfortunately, even by then the bull had long since become highly domesticated and thoroughly unsuited either for offense or defense, except possibly against another bull. Barbarians—and for some inexplicable reason this was particularly true of Iberians—soon learned that if they whipped off portions of the hides in which they were clothed and waved them at the bull, more often than not the bull would set out in pursuit of the hides and would ignore the Iberian who was waving them.

Time passed, civilization on the whole inched ahead; the Colosseum decayed and the Iberians returned to their peninsula. But the custom of waving things at bulls survived. Iberians continued to practice it, and do so to this day.

The central fact about bullfighting is that the bull is not very good at it. His problem was first formulated several centuries ago by Galileo Galilei, who said (more or less): "A bull once set in motion tends to remain in motion along a straight line." This would be perfectly satisfactory if the straight line ended at the bullfighter, but it rarely does; bulls are still passing up the Iberians and rushing at their hides.

They are encouraged to do so by a careful policy of planned parenthood, by means of which the Spanish have succeeded in breeding a race of inordinately stupid bulls who will lunge at anything that moves. Occasional deviants are culled and eaten, and only when it has been established that a given bull is harmless is he permitted to appear in the bull ring.

There, men wave red scarves at him until he has been run into a state of torpor. His spirits are temporarily revived by permitting him to chase horses briefly, while their riders jab at him with long spears. Meanwhile, the bull is being carefully studied to see if he is behaving properly. It is a deplorable fact that some bulls, although they are sincerely aiming at the red scarf, tend to miss it on one side or the other, either because they are astigmatic, or have one foot shorter than the other, or lack breeding. This constitutes a risk no bullfighter would willingly run, and is handled by the banderilleros. If a bull shows any tendency to veer to the right, for example, the banderilleros diligently hurl spikes into his right shoulder. After a bit of this he stops veering, although if he had any sense at all, he would lie down and cry.

The bull is now exhausted, bewildered, and rectilinear, and is therefore ready for the matador. Assiduous scarf-work reduces the bull to total immobility; even the sneer on the matador's face moves him no longer. The matador steps toward the bull and drops his scarf slightly; the bull, idiot to the last, drops his head to follow the scarf. He is then slaughtered, and the bullfighter is awarded those portions of his anatomy that are not worth anything, even to the bull.

This account raises a natural question: How is it that occasionally the bull manages to catch the matador in a meaty part and send him off for repairs? It is simple enough: the matador has been careless. The matador's sole duty in the ring is to make it look as if he courts danger, and now and then he is bound to miscalculate.

Basically it is all very harmless; the bull would in any case be slaughtered and eaten in the normal course of events. Meanwhile, the bullfight masquerades as an enormous display of virility, and this masquerade is frequently found convincing by frustrated women and novelists. They are aware that after the bullfight they must return to middle-aged husbands and typewriters, respectively. The women lack the self-assurance to leave their husbands, and the lovelists lack the self-assurance to leave their typewriters; so the women cheer the bullfighter, and the novelists identify themselves with him, and they all find it essential to their well-being to pretend that the whole thing is real.

and a bully portfolio by John Rombola

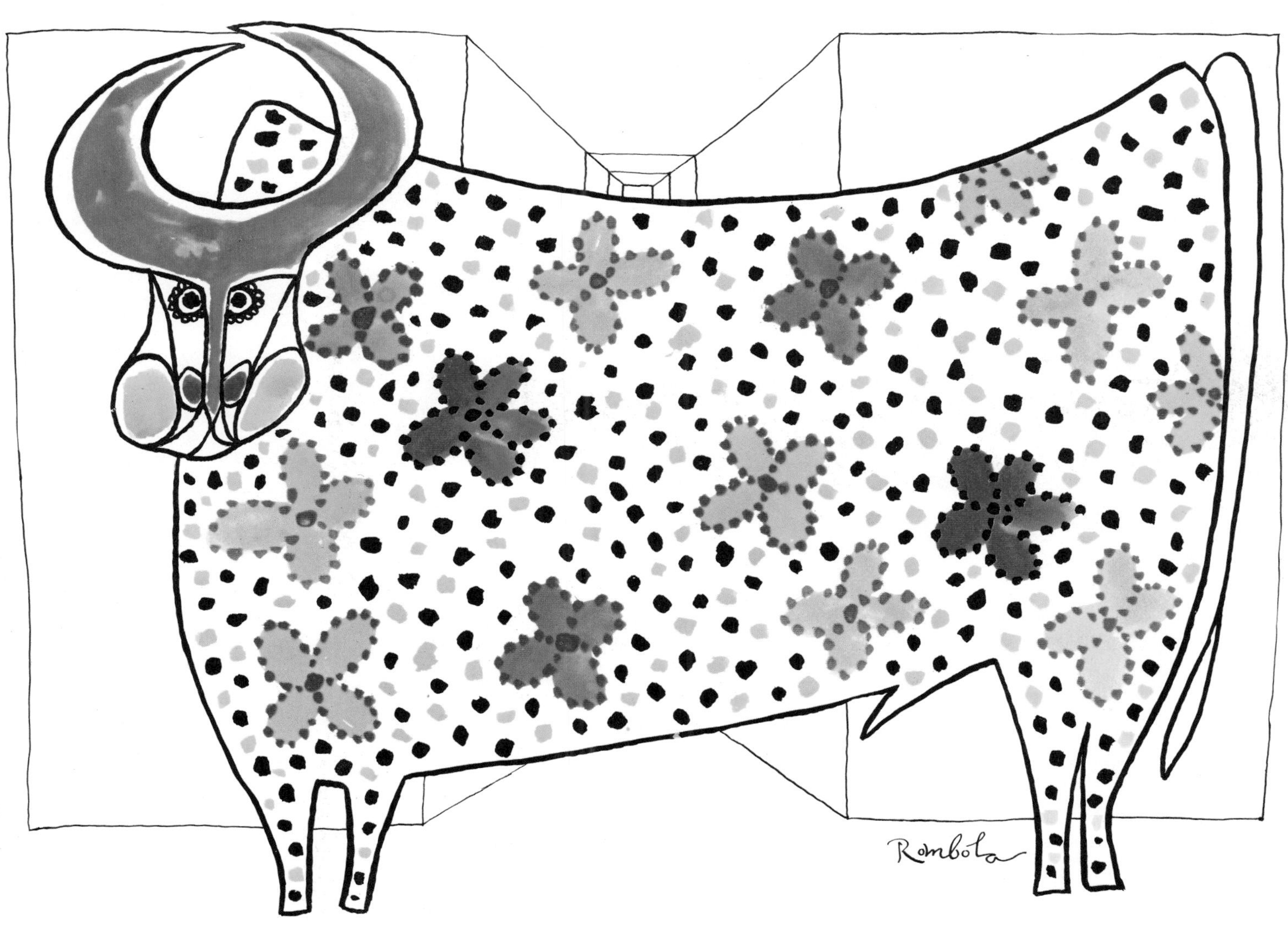

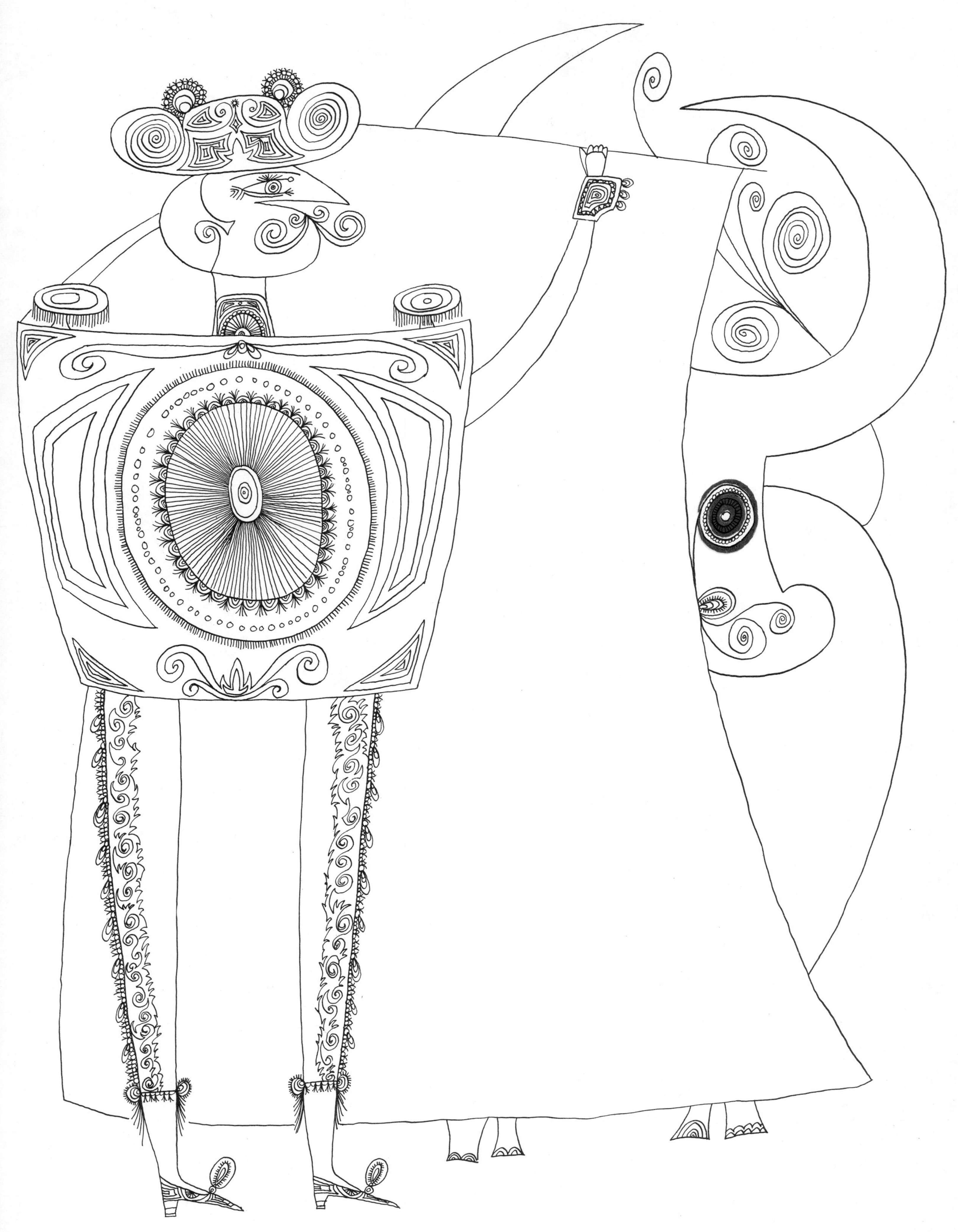